Grant scowled, holding her gaze with his. She could almost feel his anger—and his past hurts. "Dawn, I'm not easygoing or mild-mannered. I'm a black-hearted scoundrel who hasn't set foot inside a church in over twenty years."

"Actually, you've been nice most of the time. I think you're more bark than bite," she said with a small smile.

"A lot you know," he muttered, glaring at her.

She had never expected nor intended for the discussion to be so serious, but God had opened the door and she wasn't about to close it. Dawn hesitated, then took his hand in hers.

"Grant, I think your heart is like a beautiful antique mahogany cabinet. On the outside it may be grimy, even dull and black, but when it's all cleaned and polished, it will glow with an indescribable beauty. When it's unlocked and all the hurts, regrets, and guilt are cleaned out, you'll find a priceless treasure."

"Fancy words. I suppose you think you're the one to clean and polish it?" he said sharply, but he didn't pull away.

"No, that's not my job."

8/2023

Palisades...Pure Romance

Refuge, Lisa Tawn Bergren
Torchlight, Lisa Tawn Bergren
Treasure, Lisa Tawn Bergren
Secrets, Robin Jones Gunn
Sierra, Shari MacDonald
Westward, Amanda MacLean
Glory, Marilyn Kok
Love Song, Sharon Gillenwater
Cherish, Constance Colson
Whispers, Robin Jones Gunn
Angel Valley, Peggy Darty
Stonehaven, Amanda MacLean
Antiques, Sharon Gillenwater
A Christmas Joy, Darty, Gillenwater, MacLean (October)

Titles and dates are subject to change.

Palisades.
Pure Romance.

FICTION THAT FEATURES CREDIBLE CHARACTERS AND

ENTERTAINING PLOT LINES, WHILE CONTINUING TO UPHOLD

STRONG CHRISTIAN VALUES. FROM HIGH ADVENTURE

TO TENDER STORIES OF THE HEART, EACH PALISADES

ROMANCE IS AN UNDILUTED STORY OF LOVE,

FROM BEGINNING TO END!

A PALISADES CONTEMPORARY ROMANCE

ANTIQUES

SHARON GILLENWATER

PALISADES

This is a work of fiction. The characters, incidents, and dialogues are products of the author's imagination and are not to be construed as real. Any resemblance to actual events or persons, living or dead, is entirely coincidental.

ANTIQUES
published by Palisades
a part of the Questar publishing family

© 1995 by Sharon Gillenwater
International Standard Book Number: 0-88070-801-8

Cover illustration by George Angelini
Cover designed by David Carlson
and Mona Weir-Daly
Edited by Deena Davis

Printed in the United States of America

For information:
QUESTAR PUBLISHERS, INC.
POST OFFICE BOX 1720
SISTERS, OREGON 97759

95 96 97 98 99 00 01 02 — 10 9 8 7 6 5 4 3 2 1

To Ruth:
friend, neighbor, and valiant lady.
Your perseverance amazes me.
and
to Gene and Justin,
for your patience and love while I try
to get organized.
I'm so glad you can put up with fast food.

Praise be to the God and Father of our Lord Jesus Christ!
In his great mercy he has given us new birth
into a living hope through the resurrection of Jesus Christ
from the dead, and into an inheritance that can never
perish, spoil, or fade...

1 Peter 1:3-4a (NIV)

One

G rant Adams walked out of Findley's Apothecary, letting the heavy glass door slowly close behind him. Squinting against the glare of the afternoon sun, he tugged the brim of his black cowboy hat a little farther down on his forehead and looked across Main Street at Memory Lane Antiques and Collectibles. Some folks had laughed when Dawn Carson set up her shop, the first new store to open in Buckley in about five years. They said West Texas already had plenty of antiques stores, and that the pretty little blonde had been eatin' loco weed.

He walked across the cracked sidewalk to his eight-year-old pickup and opened the door, tossing the white paper sack of sundries on the seat. His gaze drifted back across the street to the license plates of the two vans parked there—one from New York, the other from California. Dawn evidently knew more about antique collectors than the old codgers who gathered every morning at Greene's Grocery for a cup of coffee, donuts, and the day's ration of fence talk. Usually the only out of state visitors who ventured downtown were lost or spending time with kinfolk.

A twinge of envy nudged him as he caught a glimpse of her through the shop window, laughing with a customer. He'd seen her smile but had never heard her laughter. Irritated with himself for being interested, he climbed into the pickup and slammed the door, only to discover that the front of Memory Lane was reflected perfectly in his outside rearview mirror. He watched as Dawn struggled to lift an old saddle from the window display.

"She has no business trying to pick that up when she's too short to reach it," he mumbled. He got out of the truck, glanced left and right, then crossed the empty street. He'd only talked to Dawn twice, maybe for a minute or two each time, and for the life of him he couldn't figure out why he kept thinking about her.

"Gonna be nothin' but trouble," he muttered, remembering the day he first met her at his friend's house, Wade Jamison. She had dropped by, looking for her cousin, Andi, who was dating Wade at the time. Dawn had been painting her store, and though she was covered with pink paint speckles and had rose pink streaks in her blond hair, she'd been cute.

Lively, too. He'd never seen a woman move—or talk—so fast. She'd hustled around the kitchen looking for something to drink and wound up cleaning out the refrigerator. Busy chewing Wade out for not calling Andi, she hadn't noticed Grant walk in and had almost run into him on her way to the front door.

He'd talked to her again the following week at a street dance held to benefit the new city museum, but since she was in charge of the whole shebang, Dawn had barely had time to say hello. She hadn't been cute that night; she'd been the prettiest little thing he'd seen in a month of Sundays.

Not only was the new museum her idea, she was ramrodding the project. There were other folks involved, but she was the driving force behind obtaining a building, funds, and items for display. Since she could charm a miser out of his last dime, he figured the museum would be the best in the area.

A little bell tinkled as he opened the door to Dawn's shop and stepped inside. Straightening, she looked up, her expression reflecting her surprise. As pleasure warmed her golden brown eyes and a soft blush filled her cheeks, the smile that had lingered in his memory lit her face. She looked cool and comfortable in a loose-fitting, turquoise knit top and jeans. He suddenly wished he'd changed shirts before coming to town instead of wearing one where the charcoal stripes had faded to dreary gray.

He glanced at the four other women standing nearby, who ranged in age from about twenty to seventy. Touching the brim of his hat with his forefinger and thumb, he gave them a brief nod. "Afternoon, ladies," he said, looking back at Dawn to include her in the greeting. "Need some help, Dawn?"

She grinned and stepped back. "Yes, please."

He plucked the saddle from the corner, lifting it over the back partition of the display case. When he turned around, the four women customers were studying him from head to toe. He half expected one of them to reach out and pinch him to see if he was real. "Where would you like this?"

"Over there." Eyes twinkling, Dawn pointed to a dark, wooden counter about ten feet behind the customers.

As he met her impish gaze, a smile tugged at the corner of his mouth. He looked back toward the counter, then at the young woman blocking his way. "Excuse me, ma'am," he said softly, slightly exaggerating his Texas twang.

The woman blinked, as if coming out of a trance. "Oh, of course," she murmured, stepping aside.

Walking to the counter, he couldn't help but overhear the

13

hushed chatter behind him.

"I don't believe it—he actually called me *ma'am*. I thought they only did that in the movies."

"I'd go see a western if he was in it. With that black hair, five o'clock shadow, and those blue eyes, he'd make a wonderful desperado."

He set the saddle down on the counter, remembering that he hadn't bothered to shave that morning. He hadn't shaved the day he first met Dawn, either. *Way to go, Adams.* Frowning, he reminded himself that it didn't matter what she thought. He wasn't interested in becoming involved with her or any woman. He'd been down that road before, dodging potholes all the way, until he fell into a bottomless pit at the end. *Then what am I doing here?*

"Do you think he's a real cowboy? I thought they wore spurs and big, fancy belt buckles."

"He's probably not. I expect most men dress that way down here to keep up the image."

"Who cares? If they all look like him, I want to stay in Texas."

Irritated, Grant tried to think of a way to leave without being rude. If he'd been anywhere else, he simply would have walked out.

"Not everyone here wears Western clothes. Mr. Adams is a local rancher," Dawn said quietly. "Spurs aren't generally needed to ride around in a pickup," she added with a smile, as she walked around the end of the counter. "And I'm sure he has several big, fancy belt buckles at home."

Her soft voice swirled around him, cooling his ire like a gentle breeze on a July evening. When he met her gaze, he saw an apology in her eyes.

"Thank you, Grant. I should've had my step stool handy. There are some old branding irons and other ranch equipment toward the back of the store. You might enjoy browsing."

"Sounds good. I'll take a look around." He smiled, silently thanking her for making his escape possible. Turning back to the customers, his smile faded. "Ladies, I hope you enjoy your visit to Texas. Let me know if you need me to carry that saddle out for you."

"Why thank you, young man," said the oldest of the women. The tiny silver-haired lady curled her hand around his arm. "Would you be so kind as to show me those branding irons? I'd like to take one home to a friend, but I want to know what the brand means. Can you tell me?"

"I'll do my best, ma'am." Grant glanced at Dawn, but one of the other women had her occupied. The old wooden floor, which had been polished to a warm glow, creaked as he and his companion made their way down the aisle. "Do you buy a lot of antiques?"

"No, but my daughter does. I have some nice things, only I got most of them before they became antiques," she said with a chuckle. She glanced back toward the front of the store and leaned a little closer. "I hope you'll forgive the girls. In my day, women waited until they were alone to talk about men." She smiled up at him and winked. "Of course, I can't blame them too much. You're the first real cowboy we've actually talked to. We've been out to California to see my other granddaughter and her new baby. Such a precious little thing."

As Grant listened to the woman prattle about her first great-grandchild, he scanned some of the items Dawn had for sale. He was surprised to see several things that looked vaguely familiar. They passed a couple who had their arms full of merchandise and were carefully examining an old cupboard. Grant remembered his aunt calling that type of cabinet a pie safe. He had one in his living room and used it for storing odds and ends.

"They're dealers," confided the elderly woman. "I heard them talking earlier about how much more they could get in California for that old lamp."

They found five branding irons hanging on the back wall of a booth filled with ranching paraphernalia. After discussing each one, the woman decided on one with a horizontal "R," which Grant explained was called a Lazy R.

The other couple had moved on, so he stopped to inspect the pie safe. It had several tin panels, which had been punctured in a simple geometric design, on both sides and in each door. He checked the price tag and blinked. Five hundred dollars. Besides the one he had in his living room, he had two others, along with a ton of other stuff that had belonged to his aunt, stored in the old bunkhouse at the ranch.

Grant carried the branding iron as they walked back to the checkout counter, where the lady made her purchase. Her daughter bought the saddle, an old bridle, and several golden-orange coffee cups that Dawn wrapped in tissue and packed carefully in a box. Grant thought he had seen some of those in a carton out in the bunkhouse, too. He hauled the saddle out to the van, wished the women a safe trip, and went back into the store.

Dawn was busy with her other customers, so he meandered around the shop, studying the merchandise with renewed interest. He found an old book written by a cowboy at the turn of the century and decided to buy it. The California dealers bought the pie safe and about ten other items. Grant helped the man carry it out and load it into the van. A few minutes later, the dealers were on their way.

"You should come around more often," said Dawn with a grin, as they walked back inside. "Those are the two best sales I've had all week."

"I didn't make any difference."

"Oh, but you did. That lady was only mildly interested in the saddle until you hauled it out of the window. She said it was worth every penny to be able to tell her friends about how you came to my rescue and how you were so charming and polite. She thought it was so sweet of you to pay attention to her mother." She met his gaze with a sincere smile. "I thought so, too."

Her perfume teased him with a soft, sweet fragrance that seemed familiar. Uncomfortable with her praise, Grant shrugged and watched as she moved around to the other side of the counter. "I have a soft spot for little old ladies," he said. "She reminded me of my aunt."

"She was a cutey. So, tell me, how did you happen to drop in just at the right moment?"

Grant felt his face grow warm, an annoying occurrence that hadn't happened in ages. "I was about to back out from the drug store, but when I looked in the rearview mirror, I saw you struggling with the saddle. You need a way to remove that back partition in the window."

She nodded. "I have a carpenter coming later in the week to change it. He's going to put some hinged pieces in so I can fold it up. I've been using my step-stool and stretching over it, but I hate not having my feet planted firmly on the floor. I get dizzy standing on a chair."

He looked around the room, his gaze skimming over several pictures and old advertising signs hanging well above her reach. "How did you get those up there?"

"A couple of the high school guys from church helped me refurbish the store and set things up."

"What do you do if a customer wants one?"

"I take a deep breath, start praying, and climb up the ladder. I can manage as long as it's leaning against the wall. I'd be silly not to take advantage of such good display space."

"Sillier to break your neck," he muttered with a frown.

"You have a point," she said, and then chuckled. "But I figure if I keep climbing that ladder, eventually I won't be afraid of it. Then I might even be able to get on a horse."

"You want to learn to ride?"

"I think it would be a lot of fun, but the one time I tried, I almost fainted. I was petrified because it was so far to the ground. Wade said I turned white as a sheet before I fell off."

"Did the horse throw you?"

She laughed and shook her head. "Nope. She was standing perfectly still. Thankfully, Wade was there to catch me. Otherwise, I would have broken something—when you fall two stories, something has to give."

Grant caught the glint of mischief in her eyes and laughed. The sound surprised him. It had been a long time since anyone other than his daughter had made him laugh. Self-preservation ordered him to hightail it out of there, but her warm, friendly smile encouraged him to stay.

Several weeks earlier, his friend Wade and Dawn's cousin Andi had gotten married. After their honeymoon, they were staying in Nashville so that Andi, a famous country singing star, could record a new album and take care of other business. "Have you heard from the newlyweds lately?"

"Talked to them a couple of nights ago. She's finished the album and is in the middle of Fan Fare right now. She spends part of the day signing autographs at a booth sponsored by the recording company and the rest of the time at a booth she and Wade set up just for her. He was griping about being cooped up in the city and that she was working too hard, but I still think he's enjoying himself."

"When are they coming home?"

"In a week or so. Wade will go completely stir-crazy if he doesn't get back to the ranch soon. Andi seems to miss it just about as much. She's really looking forward to spending most of her time there."

"She really is cutting back on her career?"

"She's had her taste of success. Now she wants to concentrate on her marriage and a somewhat normal life." Dawn grinned. "Of course, both she and Wade already have some songs in mind for her next album, and she's talking about building a recording studio attached to the ranch house. Wade said he's all for it if it means she can be home more."

Grant chuckled. "I expect he doesn't want to let her out of his sight. I'm glad they're happy. I sure hated to miss the wedding, but my daughter was in a school play that night."

"It was a nice wedding, small and quiet. Mostly just family and close friends. Wade and Andi understood why you couldn't be there, especially since they only gave us about a week's notice before they got married. How did the play go?"

"I guess okay for a bunch of nine- and ten-year-olds. The

Sheriff of Nottingham was so nervous that he almost threw up. One of the Merry Men fell off the stage but climbed right back up." He watched her eyes twinkle as she grinned. "Of course, he knocked over a fourth of Sherwood Forest in the process." His heart warmed at the musical sound of her laughter. "Robin Hood forgot part of his lines, but Maid Marion coached him through the scene. My daughter, Kim, played Maid Marion. As best I could tell, she didn't miss a single word."

"Good for her. You sound very proud of her."

"I am. She's a sweet kid. Smart, too. She lives with my mom in San Angelo."

"Wade told me. He thinks she's pretty special."

"She is." Grant wondered what else Wade had told her. *Obviously not everything, or she'd be running the other way.* He motioned toward some of the merchandise. "Where did you find all of this?"

"Garage sales, estate sales and auctions, other antique shops, and on trips back to the Midwest and Pennsylvania. Not all of it is mine. I've rented space to several dealers, but it seems like I've always been a collector. When other girls my age were asking for Barbie dolls, I was digging around attics looking for toys my grandmothers played with." She laughed again. "Now I wish I'd been a little more interested in Barbie. Those things can be valuable.

"By the time I was twenty, I had so much old stuff—and kept finding more I couldn't resist—that I decided I'd better become a dealer. That way I could enjoy different things for a little while, then sell them. I started out with a small booth in one of the shops in Sidell. My dad loaned me the money to get going, and an old family friend became my mentor. He taught me well, and within a year I'd paid back my dad and was making enough to squeak by. The Lord was good, and I found all kinds of great deals. By the end of the second year, I had booths in three shops. Soon I expanded to six."

"I think you shocked a lot of people when you opened up here in Buckley."

"Some folks are just waiting to see me go under so they can say 'I told you so.' But I'm doing all right. I bought this building for a song. I put up a billboard on the interstate and have done some advertising. Just to be safe, I kept my three most profitable booths in other stores."

"I'm impressed."

"You should be." She grinned and moved out from behind the counter, grabbing a feather duster on the way.

As she walked by, he got another whiff of her perfume. *Vanilla. She smells like fresh, homemade vanilla ice cream. Only better.*

He had the impression she couldn't stand still any longer. Nudging the brim of his hat up with his knuckle, he watched as she dusted and rearranged the items in a nearby booth.

"Could you use some more stuff to sell?"

She slanted him a glance, and he almost laughed again. He wondered how many poor unsuspecting men at garage sales had been conned with that sweet, innocent expression.

"Maybe. I'm kinda picky. Do you have something you don't want?"

Crossing his arms, he leaned back against the counter. He could play innocent, too, even though he probably had to work a lot harder at it. "Yep. Some odds and ends my aunt left me. A pie safe similar to the one you just sold and another fancier one for starters. Some other old furniture and boxes of stuff. Don't know what all is in them or if much of it is worth sellin'." A gleam of anticipation crept into her eyes, and he looked forward to seeing her expression when he opened the door to the bunkhouse. "Maybe you could come out to the ranch sometime and take a look."

"I could come out on Friday afternoon. I try to hit the garage sales on Friday mornings, but I have a clerk who works here all day."

"That would be fine. Go about fifteen miles past Wade's to the Running A Ranch. It's on the left side of the road. No fancy gate, just a cattle guard, but there is a sign. If I'm not at the house or bunkhouse, drive on down to the stable. Come any time that's convenient." He picked up the book he had left on the counter earlier. "I'd better pay for this and get going. Still plenty of work to do before dark."

Dawn came over beside him, tipping her head to read the title of the book. "I'll give you that one for making the saddle sale."

"I can't let you do that." He set the book back down, pulled out his wallet, and removed a ten-dollar bill, the marked price.

"Well, that's too bad, because I won't take your money." She fluttered the feather duster over the book and the counter, then playfully dusted his hand and the money. "There, it's all clean, so you can put it away."

He shook his head. She'd surprised him that time, and as much as part of him liked the attention, another part of him didn't like being caught off guard. That was how a man got into trouble. If he was smart, he'd tell her to forget about coming out to the ranch; he'd leave and never get within a hundred yards of her again.

Still, he ought to sell some of that old furniture if he could. It was foolish to let it sit there collecting dust when he could make some money off of it. *I'd be a bigger fool to see her again. No sense in learnin' a hard lesson twice.*

He put the money away and tucked the wallet into his pocket, moving back a step. "Then you can sell it to someone else." He turned toward the door, trying to ignore the surprise that flashed across her face and the hurt in her eyes.

Her startled look of rejection stayed with him all afternoon. It was still troubling him that night when he opened the door to the bunkhouse. He flicked on the light, his gaze skimming past various pieces of furniture and stacks of boxes to the rocking chair in the corner. How easily he could picture Aunt Lena sitting there, her fingers flying as she crocheted a brightly colored afghan or a delicate ivory doily.

He could imagine what she'd say, too. *Son, you can't bring that little gal out here to this mess. Look at all this dust. Why, the poor child will be sneezing her head off before she gets one box open. Don't you go sellin' all of it, either, Grant Adams. Your history is here.*

"I wouldn't know what to keep," he said softly. *But Dawn would.*

Weary of heart and body, he carefully dusted the old rocker with his handkerchief and settled into the chair. He closed his eyes, remembering the times he had sprawled at his aunt's feet. Though her fingers had been busy, she always had time to share his joys, sorrows, and troubles. He was in high school when his father was forced to sell the ranch. Grant thought nothing could ever hurt as much as being torn from the land and the only home he had ever known.

But he was wrong. Losing the people he loved hurt more—first his dad, then his aunt, finally his wife.

"I wish you'd been here, Aunt Lena. You would have seen what was happening and helped Susan and me straighten things out before it was too late." Guilt and sorrow weighed him down. "She wasn't really a bad woman, just lonely. If I'd been here more, maybe things would have been different. If I hadn't been so proud, maybe we could have patched things up before she died."

His gaze fell on a worn, blue cardboard box shoved beneath a nearby dining room chair, and he remembered that he had not used the bunkhouse only to store his aunt's things. He leaned over and tugged the box from beneath the chair, lifting it to his lap. With trembling hands, he pulled the top off and gazed at the contents—a boy's dreams, a man's heartache.

Dawn's customer came to mind. "You thought I should wear a big belt buckle, lady? Here's a whole box full. Take your pick." Bitterness filled him as he rummaged through the jumble of ornate gold and silver buckles adorned with angry bulls and tenacious riders. "Sorry, the big one isn't here. I got cheated out of that one."

He threw the box and lid on the floor, rubbed his hand over his face, and stared at the gold and silver trophies glistening in the light. In their present state, or even melted down, they wouldn't be of much value, but at one time they represented a significant amount of money. He'd been amazed at how much a man could earn by staying on a rampaging bull for eight seconds. With every win he had bought back another piece of the ranch.

All that he had won, all that he had gained, had not been worth the cost.

Sighing, he put the cover back on the box and picked it up. He didn't want the buckles in the house, but he couldn't leave them in the bunkhouse for Dawn to find. He turned off the light and shut the door, making a side trip to the tack room, where he hid the carton on a high shelf behind some odds and ends, away from the curious eyes of a pretty antique collector.

Unfortunately he could not bury his memories as easily.

He went to bed, leaving the window slightly open to take advantage of a cool breeze. An hour later he was still awake as the moonlight and gently swaying branches outside the window teased his imagination. He relived the moments when his life fell apart—learning of Susan's infidelity, their angry fight, and the day she moved out.

He willed himself to block out the memories. As he finally reached the fringes of sleep, the shadows on the wall became a grotesque image with fiery eyes, pounding hooves, and slashing horns. Grant threw his arm across his face to shut out the sight, but it did no good.

His mind replayed the seconds of that last ride in excruciating detail—the fall, the terror, the agony of broken bones and pierced flesh. Heart thudding, he rolled back and forth across the bed, then cried out and sat up, clutching the long, jagged scar that ran across his midsection. Panting, he fought free of the remaining fragments of the dream.

He threw aside the sheet and leaned against the headboard, catching his breath. Slowly, an even greater, deeper pain seeped into his heart and soul—the knowledge that he had lost the woman he loved. He had driven her away and had been too proud to admit that he was wrong, too arrogant to accept any of the blame until it was too late.

He took a deep, ragged breath, wishing he still had Aunt Lena to talk to. *God is always there.* Grant shook his head as his aunt's oft repeated words ran through his mind. "No, he's not. I tried calling on him once, and he wasn't home."

He leaned forward, rubbing at the ache in his knee, the one lingering injury from that ride. Propping the pillows behind him, he forced himself to think of other things—fences that needed mending, cows that needed doctoring, the good workout he had with his cutting horse earlier in the day, and a silly little joke his daughter had told him last Sunday during dinner.

Gradually he relaxed, sliding farther down in the bed, and his thoughts drifted to Dawn. *She's one sweet lady.* "And I was a jerk," he mumbled, remembering the hurt in her eyes as he rudely walked out of the store. He knew he should apologize, but he wasn't the apologizing type. He stared at the clock on the nightstand—nearly midnight.

"I wouldn't know what to say if I did talk to her." As her smiling face danced across his memory, he decided maybe it was time to figure that out.

Two

As Dawn opened the door to the store on Thursday morning, the phone was ringing. She raced to the counter and grabbed the receiver. "Memory Lane Antiques."

"Dawn?"

"Yep, it's me," she said, trying to catch her breath as she cradled the phone between her shoulder and ear, dropping her big brown purse and an armload of books on the counter.

The caller cleared his throat. "This is Grant."

Excitement spiraled through her, but she tried to keep it from showing in her voice. "Good morning."

"Did I call too early? I thought you opened at ten."

"I do, but the mayor caught me between the van and the door. Because I'm on the board for the new museum, he's been lecturing me for ten minutes on how to set up the displays, which is ridiculous since he has absolutely no idea of the work involved. You saved me once again. How are you?"

"Disgusted."

"Oh."

"With myself, not you," he said quickly. "Dawn…"

His voice trailed off, and she sensed how hard this was for him. When she first met him, he had been dressed much the same as when he came in the store, except his black hair had been a little longer and a little shaggy, and his clothes had been dusty from working with the horses. He had made her think of an outlaw that day. *Tough on the outside, tender on the inside.* "Yes?" she said gently.

"I want to apologize for being so rude yesterday. There was no call for actin' the way I did. I'm sorry."

"Apology accepted." It was her turn to hesitate. She'd spent half the night trying to figure out what she had done to cause him to turn so cold. "And I'm sorry if I offended you. I get a little carried away with teasing sometimes."

"You didn't offend me. I kinda liked your teasing." He sighed. "I'm a little rusty at all this."

"That's okay. I've got oodles of patience."

"That's not what I heard from Wade."

She detected a trace of amusement in his voice. "Oh, well, you know how he likes to stretch the truth."

"Yeah, I do."

They shared a laugh—Wade Jamison was as honest as a man could get. Dawn sagged against the counter with relief and silently thanked the Lord. "Do you still want me to come out tomorrow afternoon?"

"I'd like that." His voice dropped a couple of notes, and a little shiver of pleasure danced along her spine.

"Around two?" she asked.

"That should be fine. I'll see you then."

Dawn hung up the phone slowly, then immediately picked it up again and dialed Andi's apartment in Nashville. As she expected, they were out, but she left a message on the answering machine for them to call her.

She had several browsers and a few paying customers, but the day dragged by. Sometime in mid-afternoon, she gave up trying to do any bookkeeping and simply stared out the window.

Wade had told her a little about Grant—just enough to stir her interest and curiosity. He had attended a small country school, then transferred to Buckley High as a freshman. Although Dawn had grown up in Buckley, she hadn't known him. She was only in the fourth grade when his family lost their ranch and moved away during his sophomore year. She knew he was a widower and had a little girl, and that he had bought back part of the family ranch and wanted desperately to regain the rest. According to Wade, Grant had come very close to winning the World Championship as a bull rider, but a wreck of a ride a few weeks before the finals had ended his career and almost cost him his life.

She was aware of one problem—a big one. Grant was not a Christian. Since love could sometimes sneak up on a person, that alone should have stifled her interest. When she was younger, she had dated a few guys who didn't attend church, but she quickly realized their outlook on life was very different from hers. She had seen the problems that often developed in marriages when one partner was a believer and the other wasn't, and it seemed foolish to set herself up for heartache.

Closing the shop, she went directly home. After eating a bowl of granola for supper, Dawn stretched out on the sofa. Propping up her bare feet on the back of the couch, she absently rubbed one heel against the smooth, pale green material.

"Lord, I expect I'm worrying about things that aren't even going to happen, but I've never been so attracted to anybody. Help me keep things in perspective. I know you have a reason for getting us together. Maybe it's only for me to find more things to sell and for him to make some money, or maybe you need another person to show him your love. Whatever you have in mind, Father, please help me guard my heart and give me patience and wisdom. Don't let me go jumpin' in with all four feet like I usually do."

Most folks seemed to think she was perfectly content with her life. She had a nice income from a business she loved, was on friendly terms with just about everybody in town, and had her hand in more than enough projects to keep her busy full time. Few people realized that part of her energetic participation in church and community activities was an escape from loneliness.

Somehow, as she was growing up, it had never occurred to Dawn that she would still be single at twenty-seven. She had always pictured herself as married with a kid or two by then. Having dated several men over the years, she'd received a few marriage proposals and more than a few propositions, all of which she had declined. She had considered marrying someone simply for companionship, but those thoughts lasted about a minute. She wanted love.

Dawn didn't think she would be truly happy living anywhere else. Unfortunately, she had dated just about every eligible man around and found the relationships sorely lacking in the love department. No one had ever fascinated her as much as Grant Adams.

Restless, she went out front and worked in her flower beds until dark, pulling weeds, snipping off dead flowers, and picking a pretty bouquet of snapdragons. After scrubbing the dirt from her hands, she changed into her pajamas and curled up in a big overstuffed chair with a yellow rose print cover. Thumbing through an issue of *Antique Trader's Collector Magazine and Price Guide*, she was engrossed in an article about decorative doorstops when Andi called.

"I'd about given up on you," Dawn said, tossing the magazine on the table near the chair.

"Sorry, we've been at Fan Fare almost all day, then went out for a nice romantic dinner. Is everything okay?"

"Maybe better than okay. Grant Adams stopped by the store yesterday."

"Oh, good."

Dawn smiled and shook her head as Andi shared the news with Wade, then laughed when she heard him say, "It's about time."

"So did he ask you out?"

"No, but I'm going out to his place tomorrow to look at some antiques he wants to sell."

"Well, that's a start," said Andi. "Wade and I spent one evening with him before we got married, so I don't know him real well, but he seems like a nice guy. My sweet hubby thinks a lot of him, so he must be. Wade says he's not exactly Mr. Easygoing, though, so be prepared."

"I've already discovered that." Dawn told Andi about his visit to the store, his abrupt change from warm to aloof, and his apology. "Since he's a widower, I can understand how he might be leery of getting involved, but somehow I have the feeling there's more to it. When I flirted a little, teasing him with the feather duster, his guard went up. I was hoping Wade would tell me more about him so I don't make some stupid blunder."

"You don't want to walk on eggshells trying to please him."

"I know, and I don't intend to. I want an open and honest relationship, but if he's been hurt in some way other than his wife's death, it would help to know it. Even if I only wind up being a friend."

"You're right. He has been deeply hurt, but I think I'd better let Wade explain it to you. He once said he thought Grant would put a little spice in your life, but that you were sweet and sassy enough to handle it. I hope so."

Dawn heard some muffled words as her cousin handed the telephone to her husband. Wade had been like a big brother to Dawn for several years. He was a strong Christian, and she trusted and valued his advice. After he came on the line, she again explained what had happened. "So, do you want to fill me in, or do I have to tip-toe through the mine field on my own?"

Wade chuckled. "I don't think it would be that bad, but you're right, he has been hurt." The tone of his voice grew serious. "For as long as I've known Grant, he's been obsessed with one thing—buying back his family's ranch. That was the reason he tried bull riding. If a man's good at it—and he was—he can earn big money.

"He loved his wife very much, but he just didn't see that she needed him home more. At first she went with him to the rodeos. In fact, that's where they met. When their daughter was born, Susan decided it was too hard to keep traveling with him. She went to some of the events close by but seldom went on any of the longer trips. She was tired of the rodeo circuit but didn't like being out at the ranch any better.

"Grant was focused on winning so he could buy back the ranch, and he didn't see what was happening between them.

None of us did. She put on a good front whenever he was around.

"He lost out in the competition early one weekend and decided to head on home. Drove nearly eight hours straight, but when he got to the ranch, she wasn't there. The baby-sitter told him she was out with some fella she'd been seeing for months."

"Poor Grant. Did he ask her for a divorce?"

"No. They separated, and a week later he got hurt."

Dawn shuddered, remembering what Wade had told her about the accident. The bull had fallen coming out of the chute, wrecking Grant's knee. Unable to get away when the animal turned on him, he had been trampled and badly gored.

"He spent weeks in the hospital, then months recuperating and in physical therapy. He and Susan talked about a divorce, but it seemed as if neither one of them could take that last step. They finally agreed to see a marriage counselor, but I think they'd only been once before Susan died. She had an allergic reaction to a wasp sting and was gone before the paramedics arrived."

"Was Grant with her?"

"No. She was on a picnic with some friends. Thankfully, their daughter wasn't there."

"How old was the little girl?" asked Dawn, thinking how traumatic a mother's death would be for a child.

"Kim was four. Grant didn't think he could take care of her out at the ranch, so she lives with his mom. He and I talk about it now and then. He's worked through a lot of pain and guilt, but it's still hard for him to trust a woman. If he finds the Lord, I'd really like to see you two together. I've shared about Jesus with him, and I think he's seeking in his own way. He's a good man, Dawn, but it's not going to be easy."

"No, but I'm not going to run away. God has brought him into my life for a reason. If it's only for friendship, then I'll accept it. If the Lord has something more for us, I want to find it."

"Good for you. We'll be home in a week or so, but keep us posted in the meantime."

"Dawn's soap opera. Don't hold your breath waiting for something exciting."

As Dawn drove toward Grant's ranch the next afternoon, she relaxed enough to admire the scenery. She passed field after field with rows of bright green cotton plants separated by neatly plowed furrows of dark earth. Many of the farms had a pasture left in natural grass and mesquite trees. Some were small, only supporting a few head of cattle, but on other farms the amount of grassland appeared to equal the cultivated land.

Gradually the farm land gave way altogether to range land, wide open vistas of green grass dotted with mesquite trees, short, dark green cedar, and clumps of bear grass with long, stiff, swordlike leaves. Most of the cattle had taken up residence beneath the light green, lacy foliage of the mesquites to avoid the hot afternoon sun.

She drove past the Smoking Pipe, the ranch owned by Wade and Andi, along with Wade's aunt and uncle. The land gently rolled with low-lying hills and shallow valleys.

Then the landscape flattened out, crossed only by an occasional barbed wire fence adorned with tumbleweeds that had been borne across the prairie by winter winds. The distance between houses grew greater, making a stroll over to the neighbors all but impossible.

She drove for several miles more until a glance at the odometer indicated she was near Grant's place. Slowing a bit, she surveyed the scenery with renewed interest. For the most part, it was wide, flat prairie, broken by infrequent mesas. A gravel road cut across the grassland at an angle to intercept the highway. A quick glance in the rearview mirror confirmed that her car was the only one on the long strip of blacktop, so she slowed down even more.

Reaching the gravel road, she turned off the highway and stopped. As Grant had said, there was no fancy gate, only a cattle guard wedged securely between taut, barbed wire fences. Even the sign was a plain wooden one, simply declaring the property to be the Running A Ranch and Grant Adams as the owner.

She drove across the cattle guard, admiring the beauty of the green grass as it gently rippled in the breeze. Her gaze followed along the gravel road to the ranch headquarters approximately half a mile away, tucked at the base of the highest mesa in sight. "No wonder he worked so hard to get his ranch back. It's beautiful."

Three

❧

Grant walked out of the bunkhouse and crossed the porch, emptying the contents of the dustpan into the dirt yard. Glancing up, he spotted Dawn's blue van coming down the road, a dust storm swirling in back of her. He shook his head, figuring it was a good thing the state patrol usually ignored the lonely stretch of highway in front of the ranch. "She probably gets away with a warning every time. Just blinks those big brown eyes, gives the cop a smile, and he's putty in her hands."

Leaning the broom against the building, he tossed the plastic dustpan on the porch and hurried inside, quickly shutting the windows to avoid having to do the job over again after she drove up. When he walked back out to the porch, pulling the door closed, he saw that his worries had been for naught. She had slowed down considerably as she neared the ranch house, leaving the big cloud of dust far behind. As she approached the bunkhouse sedately, he allowed himself a small smile.

She stopped the van and turned off the engine. Leaning one arm along the open window, she grinned. "I saw you slamming those windows shut. What's the matter, cowboy? Afraid of a little dirt?"

Even as he chuckled, he wondered why it was so easy for her to make him smile. *Don't worry it to death. Just enjoy it.* She jumped out of the van. He walked down the steps, admiring the way she looked in a violet tank top, modest denim shorts, and sandals. "I've been slavin' away in here for over an hour. Didn't want all my hard work undone." He nudged his hat up slightly and looked down at her as she stood in front of him. "Do you have a regular column for speeding tickets in your monthly expense ledger?"

When she laughed, the sound seemed to ripple over him. "Nope. Don't get tickets."

He smiled wryly and shook his head. "I knew it. Those poor highway patrolmen don't have a chance."

"For your information, I'm a model citizen," she said primly, then grinned. "You just don't have a speed limit posted on your road."

"I'll have to do something about that. Are you ready to dig through some boxes?"

An excited sparkle lit her eyes. "Always."

He stepped aside, motioning casually toward the bunkhouse. "Be my guest." As she took off toward the porch, he barely kept up, but he pushed himself, ignoring the pain in his knee. Anticipation filled him when she shoved open the door and stepped across the threshold. He was right behind her.

She stopped so suddenly, he almost ran over her. Shifting a half step to the side, he watched her face as she slowly looked around the room. Her gaze caressed the mahogany chiffonier, the oak dining table and chairs, and every other piece of furniture within view. When she saw the row upon row of boxes stacked as high as her head, her eyes opened wide, and he experienced a surprisingly keen sense of satisfaction. Once upon a time the big room had been home to twelve men. Now it was filled with the accumulation of three lifetimes.

"I feel like a kid in a toy store," she whispered, "but I'll never be able to decide what to take."

"Take it all," he said, slipping his arm lightly around her.

She looked up at him, her eyes still round with amazement but now shaded with unhappiness. "I couldn't afford to buy half the furniture, much less anything that is packed away. Do you know the kind of treasures you have here?"

"No, but I'm beginning to get an idea. My aunt never got rid of anything. These are not only things she acquired during her life, much of it was handed down from my grandparents and great-grandparents."

She gasped and slowly shook her head, her blonde curls brushing the side of his chin. He was glad he had shaved.

Dawn sighed softly as if she were perfectly content to stay right where she was. "Don't wake me up. This is the nicest dream I've had in a long time."

A bud of happiness unfurled in Grant's heart, and he tightened his hold minutely. He took a deep breath, enjoying the fresh, light fragrance of her perfume. It was completely different from what she had worn on Wednesday. This, too, was unique, yet familiar. *Cucumbers? Yep. Definitely cucumbers.* He'd never met anyone like her. "You're really somethin'," he murmured.

"Yeah, I know." She looked up at him with a smile. "But you can keep remindin' me, so I won't lose my confidence."

He laughed and released her reluctantly as she eased away. "I'll keep that in mind. Now, do you want to go on a treasure hunt or not?"

"Are you kidding? I couldn't stand not going through every box here, even if I can't buy everything." She glanced around the room and her expression became thoughtful.

He could practically hear her brain whirring.

"Do you need the money right away?" she asked, turning toward him, her face bright with excitement.

"I'll take it whenever I can get it. Don't guess I'm in any rush. This stuff's been sitting here for years, and it was in my mom's garage before that."

"What if I take it on consignment? Sixty percent for you, forty for me."

Grant shook his head. His marriage had been like that, maybe even worse. He figured that in many ways he'd taken a lot more than he gave. He didn't intend to mess up again, even in a business arrangement. "Nope. Fifty-fifty. I don't have any idea of the value. You'll be doing all the work trying to sell it. Like I said Wednesday, I'm not sure how much of the stuff in the boxes is worth fooling with. Aunt Lena was kind of a pack rat. She hadn't done any home canning in several years, but we still found over a dozen boxes of canning jars. Gave them to one of her neighbors."

She looked alarmed. "Did you make sure they were just jars?"

"Yes, ma'am. I checked."

"Did you give anything else away?"

He shook his head. "No, and Mom didn't, either. She and a couple of friends packed everything up after Aunt Lena's funeral. My aunt had rented that house for almost twenty years, but the landlord only gave us a week to get her things out. There's no tellin' what you'll find together. Mom said they just tried to make as good a use of the space as they could.

"I had to get to a rodeo, so we hauled it all to my mom's place. Kept it all there until I bought the ranch." He walked over to the first stack of boxes and carried one over to the big oak dining room table. "I cleaned everything off of here so you wouldn't have to bend down so much."

"Thank you." She walked over and stood beside him. A moment later he felt her hand curl around his. "Were you close to your aunt?"

He nodded. Why did he suddenly want to keep it all? And how did Dawn know how he felt? "She was my best friend."

Dawn's fingers tightened slightly. "And you've never gone through the boxes looking for keepsakes?"

"I found a couple of things I particularly wanted, mainly because Mom had a good idea of where she had put them. Most of the furniture up at the house came from Aunt Lena's place. I never got around to looking for anything else. Never seemed to find the time."

He glanced down at their joined hands. Though hers was half the size of his, her grip was firm, with a strength that came straight from a caring heart. When he lifted his gaze to hers, her eyes were filled with concern.

"Grant, your roots are here. The things in this room are as much a part of your family history as the land we're standing on. Are you sure you want me to sell any of it?"

He brushed away her tiny frown with the back of his knuckle. "I expect I'll want to keep some of it, but believe me, little one, Aunt Lena had plenty of whatnots and things that I won't give a hoot about. And some of this is everyday stuff that you can buy at Wal-Mart. There may even be some plain old junk."

"I'll separate it into categories—antiques and collectibles, regular housewares or secondhand store items, and junk. Can you think of something in particular you'd like to have?"

"A small pair of pearl-handled scissors. Aunt Lena used them to cut her crochet thread. I'd like to keep some things for my daughter, Kim, but I don't have any idea what. Maybe you can pick out something pretty."

"Sure. You should keep some things that have a family history for her, too." Dawn slowly released Grant's hand, her gaze holding his. "Did your aunt or anyone in the family ever tell you stories about your ancestors?"

He nodded. "Both Aunt Lena and my grandpa. I'm not sure how many of them I remember."

"You'll probably be surprised at how much you've retained, especially if you see something that jogs your memory. Also, I think we should give Kim the opportunity to select what she likes. One never knows what another will find appealing."

He knew what—or who—he found appealing. A five-foot blonde with eyes that could see into his soul and a smile that turned his world upside down.

It scared him to death.

He backed up a step. "Sounds like a good idea." He walked over to the first window and flung it open, then proceeded around the room, opening them all. As he carried another box to the table, he finally allowed himself to look at her again. She was studying the stack of boxes, obviously assessing the job ahead of her. She ran her fingers through her hair, absently rearranging the casual curls. "It's going to take several days to go through all of this."

Several days of having her around. *Nice. No, risky.* "Take your time. I won't be able to help you much, but I'll try to stop by often enough to move things for you. Don't try to lift anything too heavy."

"Yes, sir." She grinned. "If it's all right with you, I'll do a preliminary sort here, then take what I think we can sell to my house for a more thorough inspection. I'll make a list for you as I go. If I run across anything I think you might be particularly interested in, I'll set it aside. Then after I go through things again, you can come by and see if there is anything you want to keep."

"That's fine with me. The fridge was taken out of here years ago, but I brought a cooler with some pop and a jug of iced tea down for you. It's over there in the corner. I'll be workin' on the water pump down at the corrals this afternoon. Holler if you need anything."

"I will. I have to get a few things from the van before I start."

"I'll move a few more of these boxes so you can reach them easier." He watched her surreptitiously as she rushed out the door, then he shifted a few more boxes to the top of the dresser and table. After adjusting a stack of boxes that seemed unsteady, he watched her trot back up onto the porch. She carried a portable radio and what appeared to be a laptop computer.

"What's the matter?" Dawn asked as she came through the door.

"I was just wondering if you ever slow down."

"I'm a snail in the morning. I have to allow myself plenty of time because I don't start functioning for a while." She set the radio and computer on the table. "I like to eat my breakfast out on the back porch if it's warm enough. Gives me a peaceful start to the day and seems to bring me closer to God."

Unsnapping the latches on the computer case, she glanced

around, then moved it to the other side of the table near an electrical outlet on the wall. After plugging in the computer, she looked up and smiled at him. "I'm gettin' lazy in my old age. This was my birthday and Christmas present to myself. Saves me a lot of time and energy. I can log everything in, then go back and put notes about the condition and possible values. I can also keep track of where I have each item—whether at my store or in one of my booths—and record sales."

"How do you determine prices?"

"I have a whole library of price guides, and I keep an eye on other dealers' prices in the shops and at shows. If I don't pay much for an item, I'll sell it for a little less than the competition, since the faster it sells, the quicker I make my money."

"Well, I'll leave you to it." As Grant walked to the door, he heard her rip off the tape on the first box. He hesitated, then turned back to look at her. "How long are you planning to stay out here today?"

"Until you kick me out or I drop, whichever comes first," she said with a smile. "I'm so excited right now, I think I could probably work all night."

"I don't usually cook much, just frozen dinners or sandwiches, but we could find something if you want to come up to the house later for supper."

"Thanks, but I brought a sandwich and some munchies."

So much for her wanting my company. He nodded. "Don't work too hard." Turning toward the door, he told himself he was better off to stay away from her anyway, but when she softly called his name, he stopped and looked back at her.

"I just meant that you didn't need to fix me anything. I'd like to eat with you."

Her sweet smile beckoned him, and her gentleness enticed him far more than any of the suggestive invitations other women had given him. A ray of sunshine pierced the cold black depths of his heart, bringing the promise of warmth and healing. "I'd like that, too. See you later."

He walked outside, carefully making his way down the porch steps so his bum knee wouldn't act up, and headed toward the corrals. A scissor-tail landed on the electric line that ran from the pole to the bunkhouse, and in the distance a calf called to its mama. Grant noticed that the day seemed brighter, which brought a silly grin to his face. He had been squinting against the glare of the sunlight since ten o'clock—it couldn't get any brighter. He felt like whistling a happy tune, but he didn't want to give the lady the impression he was glad she was there—even if he was.

CHAPTER

Four

∾⊱⊰∾

The first three boxes were disappointments, filled only with commonplace pots and pans and a nice, but ordinary, set of blue and white Corelle dishes. Dawn noted the contents on the outside of the boxes with a felt-tip pen and set them aside.

Tapping her foot to a fast-paced country tune playing on the radio, she ripped the packing tape off the fourth box and flipped open the cardboard flaps. "Yes! This is more like it." She carefully lifted out a stack of crocheted doilies in various sizes, made with fine thread and tiny, intricate stitches. Admiring the high quality workmanship, she quickly checked them for stains. All but one were without a blemish. Eight were made of ecru thread, one had a white center with a border of green leaves and clusters of variegated purple grapes, and one was various shades of pink. "The pink one may be hard to sell, but the others will go fast."

Dawn set them aside and looked into the box again, grinning at several small items wrapped in white tissue paper. "Such fun," she murmured with a chuckle and carefully unwrapped a tiny two-inch white ceramic figurine of a kitten washing its paw. "Aren't you sweet. Are you what I think you are?" Turning the kitten over, she checked for one of several distinctive stamps indicating the maker as the Ceramic Arts Studio, which created a highly collectible line of figurines and knickknacks during the forties and fifties. "Success. What about your friends, are they from C.A.S., too?"

She carefully unwrapped the rest of the items, growing happier with each one. They were all from the same company. One pair of twelve-inch tall figurines, the Lutist and Flutist, was a particularly valuable prize. There was also a pair of cowboy and cowgirl shelf sitters, about five inches high, that were especially delightful. She set those aside, thinking Kim might like them, even though she figured they might be more valuable than some of the others.

Beneath the ceramic figures was a beautiful ivory crocheted tablecloth. Dawn reverently lifted it from the box. When she was a girl, her grandmother had tried to teach her to crochet; they had both given up in frustration. "How lovely," she said softly.

The floor creaked and Dawn looked over her shoulder, meeting Grant's smile.

"She won a blue ribbon at the Texas State Fair with that tablecloth. The ribbon's probably here somewhere," he said.

"Then this should stay in the family." She set it over by the cowboy and cowgirl.

He walked up next to her. "I'd probably never use it, but Kim might like it someday." Dawn glanced up as he looked over at the figurines, his expression growing nostalgic. "I'd forgotten about all of those. I broke one once, a little horse, but Aunt Lena didn't even scold me. She didn't let me play with them after that though. Gave me metal cars and tractors instead."

"Smart lady. Do you think Kim would like the cowboy and cowgirl?"

A slow grin spread across his face as he studied them. "I believe she would. She loves coming out here to the ranch, and she has her own horse now, so she likes to dress up in western gear."

"Good. I'll leave them and the tablecloth out." She moved the items over to the top of a long sideboard. "I'll put the 'keep for sure' pile here."

"How's it going?"

"This is the first box full of treasures. The others just had regular housewares."

"Do you need some more boxes moved?"

"That would be nice. Thanks." Dawn stepped out of the way, watching in admiration as Grant carried a heavy box over to the table with apparently little effort, his flexed muscles quite nicely filling out his blue plaid shirt. When she ruefully shook her head, he looked at her with a raised eyebrow. "I tried to move that one and quickly gave up. It was just too heavy for me."

His gaze skimmed over her, and the gleam of approval in his eyes made her heart skip a beat. "I reckon bein' half as big as a minute must have some disadvantages, but I don't see any."

Her face grew warm, and she knew she was blushing. "Thanks." He stared at her with an amazed expression, and her cheeks grew even hotter. She tapped him on the upper arm with her fist. It was like hitting a rock. "What are you lookin' at?"

Grant lightly caressed her cheek, and Dawn felt his touch clear to her toes. She wondered if he noticed the goose bumps skittering over her skin.

"It's been a long time since I saw a woman blush."

Flustered, she said the first words that popped into her head. "Then you've been hanging out with the wrong kind of women."

His expression turned hard, his eyes cold. "I suppose I have."

Dawn wanted to take the words back, do anything to undo the hurt she had caused him. She reached out, barely touching his arm with her hand. "Grant, I'm sorry. I didn't mean that the way it sounded."

"Didn't you?" He pulled away.

Confused and frustrated, she looked at the floor and ran her fingers through her hair. "I don't know; maybe I did." She took a deep breath and met his icy gaze. "But I wasn't being judgmental. Just stating a probable fact." She leaned against the table and shook her head. "You rattled me, Grant."

He frowned. "Why? Because I caressed your cheek?"

"Yes."

"I don't believe it. You can't be that innocent. I'm sure other men have touched you in much the same way."

"But they weren't you," she said softly, staring at the floor again. She heard him take a quick breath but couldn't look at him as she said, "Could we cross out these last few minutes and start over? I truly didn't mean to hurt you."

Grant was quiet for what seemed like an eternity, then she felt his fingers gently lift her face until she met his gaze. He searched her eyes. "No, I don't think you did." He slowly lowered his hand and sighed. "And you're right; I haven't spent much time with women like you."

"You mean ones that don't cuss, drink, smoke, or chew?" she

asked with a teasing smile.

A tiny twinkle lit his eyes. "Yes, and who don't go with guys that do."

She laughed softly. "Well, you've got me pegged right. How about you? You don't smoke, and I don't think you chew since I've never seen you with a wad of tobacco in your mouth." Nor did he have a faded circle on the back pocket of his jeans, which was the unmistakable imprint of a can of chewing tobacco. But she didn't think it was wise to mention that. "So what about the other two?"

"I never have been much of a drinker. Don't bother with it at all now."

"Lookin' good. Three out of four, so far."

He removed his blue baseball-type cap—an advertising freebie from a feed company—and tossed it on top of the chiffonier. "I try not to cuss, so I won't mess up when I'm around Kim." He pulled off the long piece of tape sealing the next box and slanted her a glance. "But I'm far from perfect, Dawn."

"So am I." She wanted to mention that only Jesus had been perfect, but she didn't feel the time was right. She straightened and turned toward the table, helping him tug open the box top. "At least your face doesn't turn red at the drop of a hat."

"Neither does yours."

When she glanced up, he looked over to where he had thrown his cap.

Dawn laughed and playfully elbowed him out of the way. "You takin' over my job?"

"Yep. Got bored workin'. I decided I wanted to have some fun, too." He lifted a half-inch stack of newspapers from the box, scanning the dates, and dropped them on the table. "These are just packing."

Peeking inside the box, she found several cast-iron pans, but when she spotted a couple of cake molds, she squealed in excitement.

Grant jumped, then leaned closer. "What did you find?"

"It's a Griswold Santa mold." Hefting it out of the box, she checked it over.

"Like for Jello? Seems like it would be hard to get it out of that thing."

"No, it's for baking cakes, and it's only worth about five hundred dollars."

Grant released a long, low whistle as Dawn handed it to him. "Anything else in there worth that much?"

She dug around in the box. "No, but just about anything made by Griswold is valuable. We should be able to get at least forty dollars for that cornstick pan, more for the one that makes mini cornsticks, and that big old skillet on the bottom will go for a hundred and twenty-five or so." She lifted out another cake mold, this one in the shape of a rabbit. "And this guy is probably worth two-fifty or more."

"Good grief. I think I've been sitting on a gold mine."

"Yes, you have, but before we do any more digging, let me log all this in the computer." She recorded the cast-iron items first, so he could move the box onto the porch, then listed the figurines. He wrapped each one in tissue paper when she was finished with it and put it back into the box and set it aside.

He moved two more boxes to the table, then turned to her with a thoughtful frown, motioning toward the long row of cartons that were still as high as his shoulders. "You can't see over these, can you?"

"No. What's behind them?"

He rubbed one jaw and gave her a wry smile. "A wood burning kitchen stove, an old wringer washing machine, dry sink, and a dozen other things that were too big to pack or didn't need it."

"Well, don't just stand there, help me make a path." Dawn grabbed the next box from the pile, almost mashing her nose in the process, and started another stack on the floor behind her.

"You realize we're going to get trapped in here," he said with a laugh, moving another carton.

"That's okay. We can tunnel our way out." Quickly working together, they opened up a space big enough to squeeze through. Grant let Dawn go first, then grew worried when she didn't make a sound. *Guess I should have told her about the jukebox and arcade machines.* He carefully eased between the wobbly stacks to the open area on the other side. Dawn stood in front of the large floor model jukebox, running her fingers lovingly over the polished wood.

"It's a Wurlitzer," she murmured, when he stepped up beside her.

"Made in 1946. It was my granddaddy's. He staked a buddy of his in the restaurant business, but his friend couldn't make a go of it. Only lasted a year or so, partly because some fast talkin' salesman talked him into buying these instead of leasing them. Granddad took the 'toys' as payment. Said it was the best money he ever spent. He had electricity put in about the same time, and my dad said he listened to it many an evening as his parents danced."

"Does it still work?"

"Perfectly. As far as I know everything is in original condition." He plugged the jukebox cord into the wall socket and flipped a switch, lighting it up. "Pick a song. My granddaddy fixed it so you don't have to put in money," Grant said, stepping closer. "If you try a slow one, I'll ask you to dance. With this cantankerous knee of mine, I can't handle anything fast."

"I like slow. Hope I get one. I don't recognize many of these songs." She pushed a button, smiling when a mournful tune filled the air. "Well, at least it's not fast."

Grant drew her into his arms, careful to keep a respectable distance between them, though he didn't want to. "I forgot how pathetic some of these old tunes can be," he said.

"I'm not complaining." Dawn giggled when the singer sounded as if he might be calling the cows. "Not much, anyway. Guess we're used to the new country style."

"Reckon so." He pulled her a tiny bit closer and danced back and forth in the small space, smiling when her smooth temple brushed against his jaw. Once upon a time he'd been quite proficient on the dance floor. But now, with a knee that had a tendency to go haywire, he had to move carefully. "I like your perfume, but I've got to ask—is it supposed to smell like cucumbers?"

"Yes."

"So when you made me hungry for vanilla ice cream the other day, were you sending some kind of subliminal message? Did you buy stock in Greene's Grocery?"

Dawn laughed, leaning her head back so she could look up at him. "No, I found a couple of gals at a craft show in Dallas who make their own specialty scents. They were so different, I couldn't resist. Guess I have strange taste in perfume. Oh, dear, pardon the pun."

Grant chuckled, still surprised by how pleasant it was to simply be with her. "So now that I have these weird cravings for cucumbers and ice cream—"

"Better than pickles and ice cream."

"Much better. What's next?"

"Cantaloupe or lavender or spring flowers. Maybe even something exotic and sultry. I have lots of different fragrances."

They danced a few minutes longer, then the song ended, and he slowly released her. "I vote for exotic and sultry."

She glanced around and grinned. "Wrong setting. Not a palm tree in sight."

"Not quite sultry, either, but it is getting warm. I should have turned on the ceiling fan a long time ago." Grant wiggled through the maze of furniture and miscellaneous items until he could reach the cord hanging from the old fan. "Hope it works." He tugged gently on the string and the fan began to whirl.

"That's much better. There's been a breeze through the windows all afternoon, but even it has warmed up." Dawn worked her way over to the two arcade machines—a pinball machine and a big glass case that once held prizes captured by maneuvering a mechanical arm with a iron claw at the end. "Did he put these down here for the cowboys?"

Grant nodded. "He made 'em pay for playing, too, then divided the money up at the end of the month and gave it back to them so they could play again. My dad said a couple of the old-timers rarely played, but they got an equal share of the money the younger ones wasted on it. Tucked it away for a rainy day."

Dawn moved on to a Hoosier kitchen cabinet almost hidden behind the pinball machine. It had a light golden oak finish, with a porcelainized iron countertop. A flour bin and sifter, built into the top cupboard, hung above the countertop. She opened the top doors, smiling when she saw the spice rack attached to one of them. The lower cabinet had drawers on one side and two shelves on the other. Pulling the roll-front cover down over the work area, she laughed in delight. "I saw an old ad in a 1908 *House Furnishing Review* that said, 'Hoosier kitchen cabinet saves as many steps as a bicycle.' This is in wonderful condition."

"Grandma used it all the time but took good care of it. Aunt Lena took care of it, too, and only stored cook books and odds and ends in it." When she turned toward him, he thought he saw the glint of tears in her eyes.

"It's beautiful. I'd love to buy it from you. I've been looking for one to put in my kitchen for ages but haven't found one nearly as nice as this. My grandma had one, too, but gave it to my aunt. I'd loved that thing ever since I was little, but I never told anyone."

"You can have this one."

"Don't you know anything about horse trading? You haven't even heard my offer yet."

"I won't take your money." He closed the distance between them until he was standing right in front of her. "I have something else in mind." He figured she'd misunderstand his meaning. Maybe he even wanted her to, just to see how she would react. Wade had told him she was a Christian, with high morals, but he couldn't help wondering if she would revert to the age-old practice of using her feminine wiles to get what she wanted. Every other woman he had dated had tried the tactic, including the one he married.

Her face turned red but she looked him in the eye. "Don't ask, Grant," she said softly, her expression filled with determination.

"I didn't intend to, even if it may have sounded that way. I was going to propose a swap—the book I found at your shop and a home-cooked dinner or two for the cabinet." He shook his head when she started to protest. "Plus the pleasure I'll have in giving it to you. You deserve it for being willing to take on this task and put up with me in the process. Let me do this for you." He paused. "Let me do this for myself."

"You may change your mind when you taste my cooking."

"I have a feeling you're probably a good cook, as long as no one gets in your way," he said, smiling.

She laughed. "I've had my disasters, but I can usually throw something together that's decent. All right, I'll agree to your terms. I have the book in the van, but you'll have to wait a few days on the dinner. My schedule is full until Thursday."

"That's too bad. I was going to ask you to go out with me tomorrow night. Maybe dinner and a show."

"I accept," she said with an impish grin. "I have to work at the store all day tomorrow, so I wouldn't have time to fix you a fantastic meal. I think I could manage a date, though. Say around seven?"

He watched her weave her way around the arcade machines, wood stove, and jukebox. At the opening between the stacks of boxes, she stopped and gave him a wink, then pointed toward the other side and silently mouthed, "Work." As she disappeared, he shook his head. She'd caught him off guard again, triggering an automatic negative reaction, but only a minor one, and along with it came admiration for her spunk and sharp mind.

Maybe being on the receiving end of a surprise isn't always bad, he thought.

Five

On Saturday evening, Dawn opened the screen door and stepped out onto the porch as Grant walked slowly up the sidewalk. He was limping badly, and pain edged his smile.

"Did you hurt your knee?" She hurried down the steps to meet him.

"Yeah, stepped in a hole and twisted it," he said with a grimace.

"You should have called."

"I didn't want you to think I stood you up."

"I don't think you should be standing at all. Can you get up the steps?"

He surveyed the steps leading up to the high porch, then met her gaze. A tiny glimmer of humor touched his eyes. "Not without help."

"Sounds like an excuse to put your arm around me, buster." She smiled and moved next to him, slipping her arm around his waist as he draped his across her shoulders. "A nice legitimate one."

"Sometimes I like the way you think."

"Only sometimes?" As they made their way up the steps, he leaned on her, but she could tell he was trying very hard not to.

"Well, the first day I saw you out at Wade's—"

"Don't remind me."

He laughed softly, his breath warm on her temple. "I thought you were kinda cute all speckled with pink spots. And the stripes in your hair were a nice touch. I thought for a minute you were wearing the latest hairstyle."

"For the big city, maybe, but not for Buckley." Dawn eased away as they crossed the porch. When she opened the screen door, he waited for her to go inside ahead of him. "Now, what was it you were saying about the way I think?"

"I got a bit confused that day when you were talking to Wade, but I've discovered since then that you don't always talk ninety miles an hour."

"I was a little hyper."

He gingerly lowered himself to the couch, keeping his knee as straight as possible. "Yes, you were."

Dawn caught his wince of pain and quickly cleared a space in front of him on the coffee table, moving an old wooden sugar bucket filled with fluffy white cotton bolls. "You can put your foot up. It won't hurt the table a bit."

"Thanks." In an obviously well-practiced move, Grant tucked the toe of his right boot beneath his left ankle, lifting the injured leg with the good one and setting his foot on the coffee table. He shifted the other foot to the floor and leaned back against the couch with a sigh. "That's better."

"Can I get you an ice pack or something?"

"No. I already iced it a couple of times." His gaze moved over her slowly. "You look very pretty tonight, ma'am."

"Thank you." Smoothing the lightly gathered skirt of her apricot print dress, she sat down beside him. "You don't look so bad yourself," she said, noting how his bright blue shirt intensified those gorgeous blue eyes.

He shook his head. "I don't know. I think I'm gettin' too old for dating. Can't remember the last time I polished my dress boots. I was almost ready to leave before I thought about how dirty the pickup was. Got the inside cleaned out but didn't have time to wash it."

"Good. You didn't have any business washing it after you hurt your knee anyway. Do you have reservations somewhere?"

"I'm not that far gone. Called that new Chinese place in Sidell last night."

"Sounds good. I love Chinese food." She smiled as she picked up the cordless phone from the end table. "You don't happen to remember their number, do you?"

"No, why?" he asked with a slight frown.

"Because I'm going to call and cancel the reservation. We can try them some other night when you're not in misery."

"I'm okay. My knee's barely hurting now."

"Because you have it in a comfortable position. It would start hurting again after you walked down the steps, drove all the way to Sidell, and sat in a restaurant for an hour or so, right?"

"It might bother me a little, but I invited you out to dinner, so we're going."

"Nope." She dialed information and got the telephone number for the Chinese restaurant. Waving away Grant's protest, she canceled their reservation and met his scowl with a gentle smile. "I'd really rather stay here and have a pizza delivered. If we went out, I'd be worrying about you the whole time, afraid you were hurting. I'd gobble down my meal so we could leave quickly, and then I'd wind up with a stomachache. So the whole evening would be a bomb."

"You're sure you don't mind?"

"Not a bit. In fact, we were so busy at the store today, I'd welcome a relaxing, quiet evening. Would you mind ordering while I go change into more casual clothes? The number for Pizza Hut is listed in the phone's memory. Just press ten and it'll dial for you." She handed him the phone.

"What kind do you want?" he asked.

"Hamburger and black olive sounds good, but I'm not real picky. If you want something else, that would be all right."

"I'll get half of it in Canadian bacon and pineapple." He looked at the phone and the corner of his mouth lifted in a tiny, lopsided smile.

"What's funny?"

"I don't think I know anybody else who has the number for a pizza place in the phone's memory."

She shrugged. "It has space for about a zillion numbers. I just put in every one I could think of."

"And Pizza Hut came in at number ten."

"I like pizza." Dawn hopped up from the sofa and circled around the coffee table on her way to change clothes. "And I'm hungry, so call 'em already."

"Yes, ma'am."

By the time they finished dinner, Dawn had gained a bit of insight into Grant's past—not as much as she wanted, but it was a start. He had talked about his parents and his aunt, reminiscing about some of the good times they had before his father lost the ranch.

She rinsed the dishes and put them in the dishwasher while he put the few remaining slices of pizza in a plastic container and set it inside the refrigerator. "Want some chocolate ripple ice cream?" she asked. "That's all I have for dessert."

"No, thanks. I'm too full to eat another bite."

"Would you like to sit on the back porch for a while?"

"Sure." He peeked out the window above the sink. "Moon's coming up. Looks like a nice evening."

Dawn turned off the kitchen light as they went outside. The moonlight cast a silvery glow across the yard and on the edge of the porch. "There are some chairs here if you want one. I usually just sit on the steps. You can see the stars better that way."

"You sit on the steps, and I'll stretch out here," he said, easing down on the edge of the porch. Shifting, he sat sideways to the steps and leaned against a post with his legs out straight in front of him. "I always figured you'd hear a lot of noise from cars and your neighbors if you lived in town, but it seems fairly quiet."

Dawn sat down on the top step in front of Grant, listening to muted conversation coming from the house to their left and the low sounds of a television emanating from the house in front of them. "We don't have much traffic around here because of the stop signs at each block. Most folks use Elm or Sixth so they can practically go through town without slowing down. None of my neighbors have any kids still at home, so I don't hear much noise from them." Loud laughter erupted in the house next door. "Except when the Fergusons are playing canasta."

"They sound like the rowdy type," he said with a smile.

"Actually, I'm the one who has to be careful. I tend to crank up the stereo too loud when I'm cleaning house. Makes me move faster."

"I bet you wear out a mop a week. Just burn the sponge right off that little hummer." He bent his uninjured knee, placing the sole of his boot flat on the porch so his leg formed a back rest for her.

Dawn laughed and leaned back against his leg. "I'm not that fast. One every month or two is about my speed. Mopping is not my favorite chore, so I don't always do it as often as I should."

"What is your favorite chore?"

She thought a minute. "Dusting, because I get to enjoy looking at all the things I've collected. Or maybe working in the yard. I love to play with my flowers."

"You have a nice yard. Aren't those mostly wild flowers out front?"

"And here in the back, too, but you can't see them very well at night. I also have some geraniums, four o'clocks, and phlox in places and a tub of lavender."

"You really are an old-fashioned girl, even when it comes to flowers."

"I like the wildflowers because they're pretty and don't take a lot of work—except for picking off the poppies before they go to seed. I didn't know to do that the first year I planted them, and they almost took over the whole yard the next year. The four o'clocks and phlox have been here as long as I can remember. I started the lavender from a couple of plants my great-grand-mother gave me when I was about eight."

"Have you always lived in this house?"

"No, it was my grandmother's, but I stayed with her a lot when I was growing up. I loved it here and always felt safe." Dawn fell silent, remembering those troubled times.

"You didn't feel safe at home?" Grant asked gently, covering her hand with his.

"No. My dad is an alcoholic. Sometimes when he drank, he got mean."

Grant's fingers tightened around hers. "Did he hurt you?"

"A few times. Usually, Mama would send me over here if he started drinking." She clutched his hand and closed her eyes, surprised by the deep pain piercing her heart. "But if he came home already drunk, I didn't dare leave, or he would get angry and take it out on her."

"And if you stayed?"

"Sometimes he was all right; sometimes he hit me." She heard Grant's soft gasp, then felt his arms go around her as he drew her up onto the porch beside him and tenderly cradled her against his chest. Knowing the sorrow and pain he had experienced, she was moved by his ability to give such comfort. Tears stung her eyes as she wondered if there had been anyone to hold him, to ease his hurt.

"My dad's not an evil man," Dawn continued. "In a way, that made it harder. If he had been, maybe I could have hated him. He'd always been so loving and kind and fun to be with. He was the perfect daddy. I adored him.

"Then, when I was eleven, Mama got pregnant. My dad was

ecstatic. He had always wanted a son, and he hoped the baby would be a boy. Practically the first thing he did was rush out and buy a football. Seven months into the pregnancy, my mother was wallpapering the nursery and fell off the ladder. Little Jake was born that afternoon and died three days later. The doctors said he had a heart problem and probably wouldn't have lived even if she had carried him to term, but Dad couldn't accept it. He had so much hurt and anger inside that he just couldn't handle it.

"I'd never seen him with a bottle of liquor before that night. As far as I know, he'd never even taken a drink. He started drinking to bury his pain, but that only made everything worse. He blamed Mama for Jake's death, though he never said anything about it when he was sober."

"When you've mentioned your father before, I had the impression you two are very close."

"We are, now." Dawn straightened, partly because the warmth of Grant's embrace was too inviting and partly because she needed to see his face as she told him the rest of her story. He settled one hand at her waist. She toyed with the hem of her coral knit shirt, then looked up at him. "When I was sixteen, Dad's boss threatened to fire him if he didn't get straightened out. He came home drunk and in a rage. I'd never seen him so angry or so vicious. He went after my mother the minute he came through the door and knocked her down. He'd never hit either of us that hard before. I was terrified he would kill her and tried to stop him."

His hand curved firmly around her waist. "You mean you tried to stand up to him? Oh, honey…"

His endearment wrapped around her heart, and she held it

fast. "I had no choice. I thought if I could slow him down long enough, Mama could get away. But she hit her head really hard, and she was unconscious."

"So you either broke a lamp over your old man's head, or you tried to shield your mother." Grant studied Dawn's face for a long moment. "You took the beating instead of her, didn't you?" When she nodded, he closed his eyes, his face contorted with anger and pain. His fingers dug into her side. "How bad did he hurt you?"

"Broke two ribs and my jaw. Gave me a concussion."

"And you love this man? I'd like to break his neck!"

"Yes, I love him. He's not the same man, now. The neighbors called the police. They hauled him to jail and me and mother to the hospital. When Daddy understood what he had done, he was horrified and asked the judge to let him get counseling and treatment for alcoholism. Of course, he didn't want to go to prison, but he was also worried about how Mother would support us. His boss agreed to let him keep working if he straightened his life out.

"We could all tell he truly wanted to change. We didn't want him to go to prison; we just wanted him to get help. The judge put him on probation, and Daddy moved out. He went through treatment, but he was still afraid he might hurt us again. He went to counseling regularly and only came over for dinner a couple of times a week and spent the day with us on Saturdays.

"Mama had taken me to church ever since I was little, but Daddy had never gone. I'll never forget the first Sunday he went with us." She smiled and gazed up at the stars, her heart softening at the memory. "He was so nervous and afraid the church members would be mean to him. He didn't understand that when Mama and I had asked them to pray for him, we weren't asking them to condemn him but to seek God's help."

Grant moved his hand, resting it on his stomach. "So you're going to tell me he went to church and everything has been wonderful ever since?"

"No, I'm not. It took a while, and Daddy fell off the wagon a couple of times during those first few months, but he didn't come near us when he did. He went to church with us every Sunday and joined a men's Bible study one evening a week.

"Gradually, he came to understand about the love of Jesus and that God's salvation is a free gift. He didn't have to be super good or anything to receive it, and it didn't matter what he had done in the past. The Bible says that 'if anyone is in Christ, he is a new creation; the old has gone, the new has come.' When Daddy asked Jesus to live in his heart, he was like a new person. He still makes mistakes and loses his temper just like the rest of us, but he doesn't get violent. And he hasn't touched a drop of alcohol in over ten years. My folks have a very good marriage, now. They're happier than they've ever been."

Grant leaned his head against the post and stared up at the night sky for a few minutes before looking back at Dawn. "You seem like a happy person, someone who has it all together. How can you be after what you've gone through? I'm surprised you even date. Seems to me you'd want to stay clear of men."

"I couldn't have gotten through it without the Lord. I turned to him again and again for guidance. Even after I had counseling and saw the changes in my dad, I was afraid to date. But I wasn't going to let those bad experiences ruin my life, so I forced myself to go out. I chose my dates very carefully—mild-mannered and easygoing guys, usually ones who went to church. I always checked them out ahead of time if I didn't know them real well; asked other people about them. More than anything, I put my trust in the Lord to give me wisdom."

"So when did you stop being so careful?"

"I haven't."

Grant scowled, holding her gaze with his. She could almost feel his anger—and his past hurts. "Dawn, I'm not easygoing or mild-mannered. I'm a black-hearted scoundrel who hasn't set foot inside a church in over twenty years."

"Actually, you've been nice most of the time. I think you're more bark than bite," she said with a small smile.

"A lot you know," he muttered, glaring at her.

She had never expected nor intended for the discussion to be so serious, but God had opened the door and she wasn't about to close it. Dawn hesitated, then took his hand in hers.

"Grant, I think your heart is like a beautiful antique mahogany cabinet. On the outside it may be grimy, even dull and black, but when it's all cleaned and polished, it will glow with an indescribable beauty. When it's unlocked and all the hurts, regrets, and guilt are cleaned out, you'll find a priceless treasure."

"Fancy words. I suppose you think you're the one to clean and polish it?" he said sharply, but he didn't pull away.

"No, that's not my job."

"No? Aren't you out to save my soul and me from myself? Don't you see me as just some kind of reclamation project?"

"My faith is very much a part of me, Grant. It's natural for me to want you to have the joy and peace I have in Jesus, but a woman can't change a man." Thinking of his wife, she added,

"And a man can't change a woman. Only the Creator can." Wanting to ease the tension between them, she grinned. "Of course, I might take my feather duster to you now and then."

Slowly, a tiny smile chased away his frown. "Are you always so honest and direct?"

"Always honest; not always so direct."

Grant turned his hand over, clasping Dawn's, and tugged her a little bit closer. "If you had any sense, you'd tell me to leave and not come back."

"Then I wouldn't get to go on a treasure hunt in the bunkhouse."

"So you're just interested in my junk." He released her hand, sliding his arm around her and drawing her closer still.

She rested her hands on his chest. "I wouldn't say that," she whispered, as he put his other arm around her.

"Bad boy. Good girl. Aren't you afraid you're asking for trouble?"

"No. You may look like a handsome desperado sometimes, but I don't think you're so bad." She smiled. "Wade wouldn't have encouraged me to go out with you if you were." Surprise flickered across Grant's face, and she eased her hands up to his shoulders and looked into his eyes. "I trust you."

"I'm not sure you should, but I'm glad you do." He slowly lowered his head, touching her lips with such tenderness that it brought tears to her eyes. "So sweet," he murmured, wrapping her in his strong embrace, kissing her deeply.

Dawn had never experienced anything so beautiful. When he finally raised his head, she slowly opened her eyes and stared up at him in wonder.

He looked shaken. After a few seconds, he glanced up at the sky. "Uh, nice moon."

She laughed softly. "I noticed it when we flew by."

He met her gaze and smiled. "Guess we'd better just look at it from down here."

She nodded and turned around in his embrace so she could lean back against his chest. "Safer," she said, thinking how long she had yearned for a man whose kisses sent her soaring to the heavens. Suddenly, she pictured them trying to navigate through all sorts of space debris.

When she giggled, Grant tilted his head and looked down at her. "You find my kisses amusin', Ms. Carson?"

"Not in the least, Mr. Adams. I was just imagining us being bumped by that satellite." She pointed to the rapidly moving pinpoint of light high in the sky.

Grant laughed softly, resting his chin on the top of her head.

Dawn entwined her fingers with his and breathed a quiet sigh of pure contentment. *Draw him to your love, Lord.*

Dawn's part-time clerk, Emily, was happy to take care of the store on Monday, leaving Dawn free to work on the project at Grant's. When she arrived at the ranch at nine-thirty, Grant was already hard at work mending a section of barbed wire fence along the highway. She pulled off the pavement into the shallow, dirt bar ditch and turned off the engine. Hopping out of the van, she sauntered over to his side. Grant's cap hung on the top of a nearby post, and in the sunlight, his dark hair shone like polished ebony.

"You look awake and raring to go," he said with a smile of greeting.

"Yep. Been up since eight and functioning reasonably well for the last hour."

"Eight! Day's half gone by then. I've been out here since six-thirty. Some of the cows decided to go visitin' their friends up the road and knocked down the fence. About the middle of my second cup of coffee, I spotted them meandering along the highway."

Dawn patted him on the arm. "Such a hardworking man."

"That's me. No time for play or flirtin' with pretty ladies." Holding a handle of the posthole digger in each hand, he shoved the end into the ground, standing it upright.

"You really look like a man in a hurry."

"Well, even a hardworkin' man has to take time out for a drink of water." Grant held out his arm as if he were escorting Dawn into a grand ballroom. "Care to join me, ma'am?"

"I'd be delighted." She curved her hand around his arm and walked beside him to the pickup. Releasing his arm, she leaned against the truck as he tugged off his heavy leather work gloves and laid them on the hood, then pulled a gallon thermos from the shade beneath the vehicle. He offered her a drink, but she declined with a shake of her head. "No, thanks. I'm still cruisin' on coffee. Did Kim come home with you yesterday?"

Grant nodded, then took a long swallow from the open jug, wiped his mouth on his lightweight chambray sleeve and put the stopper back in the thermos. "I expect she's still asleep, or maybe watching cartoons. I told her you'd be out today." He set the thermos back underneath the truck. "She'll probably come down and pester you. If you don't want her there, just tell her so. I told her not to be a bother."

"I'll enjoy the company."

"But you might not get too much work done. That kid can talk a blue-streak when she's in the mood, or ask a hundred questions in ten minutes." The warm glow in Grant's eyes reflected his love for his daughter. "Thing is, most of what she has to say is interesting."

"Kids nowadays have more going on than we did; they live in an electronic world."

He nodded. "She's a whiz at Nintendo and was learning

about computers at school this year, but she still notices the little things, too. Has a real interest in nature. Makes me stop and appreciate the everyday flowers and birds I tend to take for granted sometimes."

"I look forward to meeting her," Dawn said. "I'd better get going. There's still plenty to do."

Grant picked up his gloves and walked with Dawn back to the van, cupping her elbow to help her up onto the seat, then shut the door. Reaching through the open window, he flicked a small bug off her shoulder and out the window. "I should finish here shortly. I'll drop by the house and see if Kim is up. Probably take her with me to check the cattle on the other side of the ranch. At least I'll strongly encourage her to go so you can have some quiet time to work. I'll be practicing with my cutting horse this afternoon, so Kim will probably bounce back and forth between us to keep occupied."

"Whatever. I like kids. Probably because I act like one half the time myself." She placed one hand on the steering wheel and reached for the key with the other.

"Only half the time?" he asked with a mock expression of innocence.

"I can be very mature," she said primly, then pretended to be puzzled. "I think."

Grant leaned down, resting his forearms on the window. "There are moments when you're all woman, that's a fact."

Dawn felt a blush flood her face but couldn't think of a quick or clever response, not with him so close or looking at her the way he was. She dropped her hands to her lap, resisting the urge to weave her fingers through his.

Grant traced the warmth in her cheek with the tip of one

work-roughened finger, then straightened, slowly lowering his hand to the window frame. "Come up to the house for lunch. I stocked up yesterday."

"You mean you have something besides bologna?"

He nodded solemnly. "Peanut butter and jelly, a variety of turkey,...as well as bologna and the biggest package of Oreos they had."

"Sounds like Kim helped you shop."

A twinkle lit his eyes. "You got it. See you later."

"When you hear the rumble of a hungry stomach, you'll know I'm on my way." Dawn started the van, waved, then pulled back onto the highway, driving the short distance to the ranch entrance.

She worked hard all morning and made good progress, finding many things to take to the store and her other booths. Some wouldn't bring high prices, but they would probably sell quickly, so they were beneficial due to the short turnaround time. Others fell into the mid-price range, and several were higher value items way beyond the scope of her shop. She planned to ask her mentor in Fort Worth, who had contacts all across the country, to take them on consignment.

At noon she walked up to the ranchhouse to join Grant and his daughter for lunch.

Grant smiled at Dawn through the kitchen window as she stepped on the porch. A second later he pushed open the screen door. "Hi, pretty lady," he said softly.

"Hello." She smiled at him, feeling ridiculously thrilled at his words and the light in his eyes. "Hope I didn't keep you waiting."

"Just puttin' stuff on the table." He held the door for her, then eased it closed after she walked by.

His daughter watched them closely as she set the mustard and mayonnaise on the table. Kim was a pretty girl, with Grant's black hair and deep blue eyes, but otherwise there was little resemblance. Dawn didn't think Kim could have braided her hair so neatly, and she pictured her standing in front of her daddy, his big hands plaiting the long locks with gentle precision. It was an endearing image.

"Dawn, this is Kim, my pride and joy. Kim, this is my friend, Dawn Carson."

They exchanged greetings, then Kim grinned at her Dad. "You're right. She is pretty."

Grant blinked and turned a little pink, then laughed and hugged Kim with one arm. "See what I mean?" he said, looking at Dawn. "The kid keeps me on my toes."

Kim hugged him back and shrugged. "Somebody's gotta."

"Looks like you're doing a great job," Dawn said, instantly liking the girl.

"Don't encourage her," said Grant, tugging playfully on Kim's long braid.

Grant and his daughter bantered throughout lunch, including Dawn in their fun. She was touched by their obvious love for each other and thought it sad that Kim couldn't live at the ranch all the time. She kept her opinions to herself, however, since she didn't think it was her place to say anything.

When they had eaten and washed the dishes, Grant plucked his straw hat from a hat rack by the back door. "I'm going to be working with Dancer. Kim, do you want to ride down to the cutting pen with me?"

"Could I walk down later? I'd like to see some of Aunt Lena's stuff."

"You'd better ask Dawn if it's all right with her."

Kim looked hopefully at Dawn. "May I come watch you, Miss Carson? I promise I won't bother you."

Behind Kim, Grant raised an eyebrow, his expression amused.

"Sure, but I might put you to work," Dawn warned, with a smile.

"I don't mind," Kim said quickly. "I'll be glad to help."

Dawn thought she probably would. She had certainly pitched in without any protest to prepare lunch and clean up afterward. "Good, but we'll try to make it fun. Why don't you call me Dawn?"

Kim looked at her dad for approval. When he nodded, she grinned. "Okay, Dawn."

"Come on down after a while, Kim, so you don't wear out your welcome," Grant said.

"Yes, sir. I want to watch you and Dancer. Have you seen my dad ride his cutting horse, Dawn?"

"No, not yet."

"You'll have to go with me. They're really somethin'."

Dawn looked at Grant, smiling at his pleased expression and remembering the first day in the bunkhouse when he had said the same thing to her. "I'm sure they are," she said, her gaze locking with his.

He stared at Dawn for several seconds, then cleared his throat and slipped on the dusty, well-used hat. "See y'all later."

Dawn and Kim told him good-bye, then walked down to the

bunkhouse, with the girl asking questions about the antique business all the way. "I really like those little cowboy and cowgirl figurines. Thanks for saving them for me. I have them sitting on the shelf above my desk. Are they worth much? Daddy didn't know."

"Yes, they are. I checked a couple of price guides yesterday afternoon. They would probably sell for about seventy-five dollars for the pair."

"Wow! I sure won't let my friends pick them up. They'll just have to admire them from afar," Kim said, with her nose in the air and a toss of her long black braid. Then she giggled. "I haven't got the snooty accent down."

Dawn laughed, opening the screen door to the bunkhouse. "You did well with the haughty expression, though. What did you think of the tablecloth?"

"It's really pretty, and Aunt Lena was so special to Daddy that I'm glad I'll have it when I'm grown. He put it in a trunk at the house with some things of my mother's that he's saving for me."

"Good. If you see anything else you want, let me know and we'll set it aside. Your dad gets final approval, okay?"

Kim nodded, then walked over to the table, inspecting but not touching the various items Dawn had left out. "What's this?"

"A coffee mill. It's okay to pick it up and look at it. Back before people could buy ground or instant coffee, they bought the beans and either ground them at home or had them ground at the grocery store. There are some stores that still sell hand-crank coffee mills instead of electric grinders."

"Grandma sometimes buys special coffee beans and grinds them at the grocery store with the big electric grinder. She bought a little electric one to use at home but decided it was too messy. She usually just buys coffee in the cans."

"Me, too. I'm not a coffee connoisseur. Just give me something that tastes decent and has caffeine, so I can wake up in the mornings."

Kim turned the crank, then pulled out the little drawer on the side. "You put the beans in the top and this is where it comes out when it's ground?"

Dawn nodded and sat down at the table to enter the items into the computer log.

"What's a connos—what was that word you used?"

"Connoisseur. It means an expert or someone who can appreciate subtle differences in things, like the different flavors of coffee or different pictures in an art gallery."

"I'll have to remember that one. It sounds important. What are you doin' now?"

Dawn explained about logging in the merchandise and how much easier it was to keep track of everything on the computer. This led to a discussion about the things Kim had learned on the computer in her classroom the past year. They went through more boxes and found many additional things to sell. Having Kim working with her slowed down the process, but Dawn enjoyed the girl's company and her honest interest in what they found.

"I don't think my mom liked anything old," said Kim, as she held the box still while Dawn carefully replaced a tissue-wrapped cut glass bowl inside. "Everything I have of hers is modern—pictures, vases, dishes. Things like that. My grandparents—her folks—have all modern furniture, funny looking pictures, and weird lamps. They've got a cool big-screen TV, though."

Dawn walked over to the ice chest in the corner. "Want a pop?"

"Yes ma'am. Got an orange?"

"One orange coming up." Dawn took out a grape soda for herself and walked back to the table. Handing the pop to Kim, she sprawled on a dining room chair. "Let's take a break. It's too hot to work so hard."

Kim agreed and sat down, opening her drink.

"Do you see your mother's folks often?"

The girl shook her head. "Not too much. They live in Denver. I usually go up for a week in the summer." She made a face. "A week's long enough. They're always havin' fancy parties or goin' some place where you have to get all dressed up."

"You don't like to dress up?"

"It's okay on Sundays for church, but I had to wear this real expensive, fancy lace dress for Grandma Rochelle's party last year. She must've told me a hundred times to be careful and not spill anything on it. I was scared to eat or drink anything. I about starved. And my shoes were too tight."

"But you didn't dare take them off, right?"

Kim nodded. "Grandpa is neat. We played miniature golf and then got hamburgers, and he took me to the zoo. I guess Grandma isn't so bad really, except she worries too much about me gettin' dirty and stuff. She says I'm too much of a tomboy and should dress and act more ladylike. She tells me lots of stories about my mom, though."

"Do you remember your mother?" Dawn asked gently.

"Not much. I remember her reading me stories at bedtime and then rockin' me to sleep. Oh, and I remember her making me peanut butter and jelly sandwiches 'cause she'd cut off the crusts and cut the sandwich into little squares. Grandma had some like that at her party, only they weren't peanut butter and jelly. Seems like Mom liked parties, too. She was beautiful, but I'm not sure if I really remember that or have just looked at her pictures a lot. I have a bunch of pictures of her. She was almost as tall as Daddy with long blonde hair and green eyes. Grandma, my dad's mom, says I look a lot like her except for my hair and eyes."

Dawn smiled and nodded. "You favor your father there. It's a very nice combination."

Kim studied her for a minute. "You like my dad?"

"Yes, I do."

"You want to marry him?"

Dawn choked on a swallow of soda. When she quit coughing, she wiped the moisture from her eyes. "It's a little soon to be thinking about that. We've only had one date."

Kim's eyebrows shot up, and she sat up straight as a board. "You had a date with my dad? He actually took you out?"

Oops. "Well, not exactly. We were going out to dinner, but he hurt his knee Saturday, so we just ordered pizza and ate at my house."

"Then what did you do?" Kim leaned forward, resting her elbows on the table. Dawn couldn't tell if the girl was excited or upset.

"We sat out on the back porch and talked."

Kim sat back with a grimace. "Bor-ing."

Not hardly. "We haven't known each other for very long, so it was nice to get better acquainted."

Kim frowned and crossed her arms, looking Dawn straight in the eye. "I've got a friend who says her mother's boyfriend stays at their house every weekend. Did Daddy spend the night with you?"

Good grief! When did ten-year-olds become so direct? Or learn about such things? On reflection, Dawn realized she'd been somewhat tuned in to these matters by the time she was eleven. Maybe even sooner. "No, he went home around ten-thirty."

"So you didn't sleep with him?"

"No. I don't believe in sex before marriage, and your daddy was a gentleman."

Kim's frown disappeared and she visibly relaxed, focusing on the small gold cross on Dawn's necklace. "Do you go to church?"

"Yes, to Buckley Community Church. How about you?

"We go to First Baptist. Grandma takes me every week. I'm in a great Sunday school class. Are you a Christian?"

"Yes. I gave my heart to Jesus at camp when I was about your age."

Kim's broad smile lit her whole face. "Me, too! Last summer."

"That's wonderful." Dawn reached across the table and squeezed Kim's hand. Sitting back, she asked, "Does it bother you that your Dad and I had a date? Or may go out again?"

"No, ma'am. Grandma and I worry about him being out here all by his lonesome. She's afraid he's going to become a hermit." Kim laughed. "We'd been studying about hermit crabs in school, and at first I thought she meant he was going to become a crab. I told her he was already crabby sometimes, so she had me look *hermit* up in the dictionary so I'd understand." Kim grew somber. "As far as I know, you're the first woman Daddy's really dated since he and Mom split up. I think he likes you a lot."

Dawn's heart skipped a beat. "Oh? What makes you think that?"

"Because he watches you all the time, even when you're not

lookin' at him." She smiled. "And he talked about you when he came to get me yesterday—talked about you a lot. Grandma noticed, too, but she didn't say anything to him. I didn't, either."

"You won't razz him about taking me out, will you?"

An impish expression filled Kim's face. "Not too much. Let's go down and watch him and Dancer. You just gotta see them."

Dawn agreed, and as they walked toward the cutting pen, Kim told her about the important cutting competition Grant had entered the previous November. "The Futurity is the biggest cutting event there is. Only a three-year-old horse who's never been in competition for money can enter. Practice contests are okay. In fact, you have to go to some, because if you don't the horse will be too scared by all the people and noise to do anything.

"They have non-pro and open categories. The non-pro is for people who haven't earned any money for actually training horses, so everybody thought Daddy would enter that one. But he didn't. Anybody can enter in the open category, and a lot of people give it a try, but usually just the professional trainers take the top places or even make the finals. Daddy went for it because that's where the big money was."

"How did he do?"

"He placed third! Nobody could believe it. There's been a few non-pros that even won it, but not very many, and usually their horses came from a long line of winners. I heard a bunch of people talkin' about how unusual it was for a non-pro rider and an unknown horse to do so good. He won over sixty-five thousand dollars."

"My goodness! That's a lot of money." Dawn thought of Grant's home, which wasn't exactly run down but could use some repair. There was one new building, a small stable next to the corrals, but the barn and other buildings needed a paint job. His pickup was several years old, dented here and there, and sounded as if it had a cold whenever he started it. She suspected he had spent the money on more land instead of improvements. "How nice for him to do so well. I'm sure he worked hard to make it happen."

"He really did. He took Dancer to a trainer for a while, but mostly trained him by himself. When Daddy figured out that Dancer was pretty good, he built the stables so he could take better care of him. Our other horses stay in the barn and corral or out in the pasture. Course he lets Dancer go out in the pasture some, too."

"How many horses do you have?"

"Four, counting Dancer. Daddy uses Gus for herd holding at the competitions and general ranch work. He calls Smokey his do-anything horse, and Mitzie is mine.

"After we came home from the Futurity, Daddy took me to Disneyworld and Universal Studios. We even went swimming in the ocean. And he fixed up Grandma's car—new transmission and tires. He bought a new bull and with what was left, he bought back some more of the ranch."

"Is he getting ready for another competition?"

Kim nodded vigorously. "The Derby. It's held in Fort Worth, too, in July. It's for four-year-olds and doesn't pay as much money as the Futurity, but if he wins, he could still get a bundle. At least that's what he said. I don't know how much he really meant. Someday, if Daddy can keep winning at big payin' events, he's gonna own every acre that belonged to Great-Grandpa."

With her deep sense of history and love of family, Dawn understood Grant's need to reclaim the family land. Roots ran deep in this part of the country.

"He'll be workin' in the arena today 'cause it's more like the one they use in competition. It's square, where the other pen is round. You use both to train a cuttin' horse."

As they approached the large pen, Grant was perched atop his horse, quietly walking through a herd of about ten good-sized calves. Dawn noticed that the lower half of Dancer's tail had been braided. *So that's why he did so well with Kim's hair.* "Why does your dad braid Dancer's tail?"

"So he won't step on it and break off some hair when he's making a low, quick turn. Daddy always braids it for practice to keep it nice for competition. When they're done, he loosens it and gives him a bath." She grinned. "He puts my hair conditioner on Dancer's tail and mane to keep out the tangles. He clips the hair short where the bridle goes and trims it on his face. Says Dancer looks like a shaggy dog if he doesn't."

Two other horses in the arena were tied in each corner on the same end as the herd. "Why are those other horses in there?" Dawn asked in a low voice.

"They act as herd holders. Keeps the herd from moving around too much. It works pretty good when Daddy doesn't have Wade or Neil to help him. That's Gus on the left and Smokey on the right."

"Who's Neil?"

"He works for Daddy part time, when Daddy needs some help. Neil has a small place between here and Wade's. In competition, a couple of riders help keep the herd where they're supposed to be. Two more men—or sometimes women—are on the other end. They're called turnback men, and they keep the cow from runnin' off to the far end and just running up and down the fence."

"Wade's never mentioned helping in a competition. Does your daddy take people with him to help?"

"No," said Kim with a shake of her head. "Most of the time folks who are competing just help each other. Daddy takes Gus with him to help out. Nobody uses their cutting horse for herd holding."

Dawn had never seen a man who looked more at home in a saddle, although Grant seemed to slump a little more than others she had seen ride. He held the reins in one hand and loosely gripped the saddle horn with the other.

He really is the perfect cowboy, Dawn thought. A man of honor, with a deep respect for those who came before him. A man who truly finds happiness in the land and the freedom of open country. She thought of the love and closeness he shared with his daughter, even though they didn't always live together. If ever a man needed hearth, home, and family, it was Grant.

They watched as he guided Dancer, silently separating several calves from the herd, driving them toward the middle of the pen. He was obviously focused on one calf in particular, letting the others drift around him to go back to the herd. When the black calf was all alone in the middle of the pen, Grant tightened his grip on the saddle horn and lowered his rein hand in front of the saddle.

The horse and calf stared at each other for a few seconds, both alert with their ears pricked up. The calf suddenly seemed to realize she was all by herself and cast a furtive glance at the herd. She trotted left, trying to get back to them, and Dancer instantly jumped to block her way. Back and forth, from side to side—sharp, quick turns, little runs, and deep sliding stops. Dancer faced the calf, seeming to dare her to try again. The calf darted right, and once more the horse thwarted her run toward the herd. Dancer moved with grace and power, his bright eyes shining with intelligence and pure enjoyment.

During the whole encounter, Grant had not picked up the reins or said a word. Touching the horse lightly with his spurs a couple of times had been the only visible instruction to the animal. Grant seemed to concentrate on staying in the saddle, moving with the horse, and enjoying it.

Not for the first time, Dawn felt a twinge of envy for someone so at ease on a horse. She'd always thought it would be wonderful to gallop across the prairie, to feel free as the wind. *Wish you made horses a little lower to the ground, Lord. Or I wish I'd learned to ride when I was eight or nine. I wasn't afraid then.*

Grant and Dancer played with the calf for a couple of minutes, then he lifted the reins and turned the horse away, letting the cow skedaddle back to her companions. He looked up and smiled, first at Kim, then at Dawn. The warm welcome in his eyes made her weak in the knees.

Please God, let him come to know his Savior soon. Otherwise, I'm going to have to make myself scarce around these parts before I go and fall head over heels in love.

Seven

❧

As Grant passed Kim's bedroom that night with an armload of freshly folded towels, he heard her talking. Thinking she said something to him, he paused outside her partially open door.

"Thank you, God, for a really good day."

With only filtered lamplight from the living room illuminating the hallway, Grant knew Kim couldn't see him standing behind the door. Tenderness welled up in his heart as he listened to his child praying with innocent simplicity, and he regretted all the times he had put her to bed with only a kiss and a hug. He had never prayed with her. He wasn't even sure if he'd ever thought about it.

Grant remembered how his mother had faithfully sat on the edge of his bed each night and prayed with him. She'd stopped when he was eight, when he had told her he was too big for her to tuck him in. A few years later, he had decided that since his dad didn't go to church, he wouldn't go, either.

He turned his attention back to Kim as she continued to pray. "It's so nice to be out here with Daddy. I love Grandma, and it's nice to be able to run over to Jenny's and play, but it's so much fun here on the ranch. I wish I could stay here with Daddy all the time. I love him so much."

Grant's eyes stung, and a thick lump instantly formed in his throat. *I love you, too, sweetheart, but I can't take care of a little girl way out here by myself.* He swallowed hard and blinked back the moisture in his eyes.

"Dawn's really neat. I hope Daddy keeps dating her 'cause he smiles more than he used to."

Grant found himself smiling and shaking his head, wondering how the little imp learned about their date. *Probably asked Dawn straight out and gave her the third degree.*

"And, Jesus, please help Daddy to understand about you. You're an awfully good friend to have. I just know if he believed in you, he'd be a lot happier."

Suddenly irritated, Grant tiptoed barefoot down the hall to the bathroom and put the towels away in the linen closet. *Yeah, right. Just believe in Jesus and all your problems will disappear. Sorry, kid, but in the real world it doesn't work that way.* Yet he couldn't help but hope Kim's world would be different. He hoped she never made mistakes that would haunt her for the rest of her life or experienced betrayal by someone she loved. Or even worse, lost that person, knowing she could never make things right.

He waited a few minutes before going quietly back to the living room. Turning on the television and muting the volume, he flipped channels for a couple of minutes before shutting it off again. A stack of magazines and newspapers on the table beside his recliner drew his gaze, but he was too restless to even pick one up. As he wandered out to the front porch, Kim's prayer nagged at him.

He thought about the people for whom he cared the most, as

well as acquaintances he liked and respected. Many of them were Christians. His grandparents and great-grandparents hadn't talked about God much, but they were the finest people he had ever known. Looking through the front window, his gaze fell upon his grandfather's Bible in the bookcase. A book didn't become as worn as that unless it was handled often. Grant had tried to read it a couple of times when he was feeling particularly lonely and vulnerable, but it hadn't made much sense. He blamed it on all those "thees and thous" but supposed it actually had more to do with his attitude.

He and Kim had once had a discussion about whether there was a God or not. "It's easier for me to believe there's a God who made everything than to believe a bunch of energy just went *ka-bam* and life was formed," she had said.

He had to admit he agreed with her.

When she came back from church camp last summer and told him about accepting Jesus, her face had glowed and a new light glistened in her eyes. "I don't really understand how or why it all works the way it does, Daddy. I just know I feel happy and different on the inside."

Grant sat down on the porch step, gazing out at the prairie bathed in moonlight. His friend Wade believed in Jesus with unwavering faith, but that hadn't always been the case. When Grant first met him on the rodeo circuit, Wade was right out of high school and a bitter, angry young man, the product of a prosperous but deeply troubled home. He was a bull rider, too, but he didn't stay with it long, for which Grant was thankful. There were times when he sensed his buddy would just as soon have been trampled to death as win.

Grant leaned over and picked up a pebble, tossing it farther out into the yard. Their friendship had remained strong even after Wade left the rodeo, and a few years later, Grant noticed him begin to change. Over time, Wade's bitterness and anger disappeared. He mellowed out and laughed more often. Perhaps even more important, most of the time he seemed at peace, where before, he'd always seemed at war.

Grant finally asked Wade what brought about the changes in his life. His friend was quick to give a good deal of credit to his aunt and uncle and their love for him. Then he told him about finding Jesus. Grant was surprised but figured if gettin' religion helped his friend, then he wasn't going to put him down for it. Grant was even a little curious, although not enough to do anything about it. But when he came home and found Susan out partying with another man—and in a relationship that involved more than a night on the town—he decided that if there was a God, he didn't care one whit about Grant Adams.

Now he wasn't so sure. It seemed as if he were surrounded by people who believed in Jesus. Good, kind, loving people who cared about him. He knew his mother prayed for him every day, and she rarely missed an opportunity to tell him that God loved him. Over the years, Wade had stood by Grant through all his troubles, never finding fault, even when pointing him toward the truth. Wade had often spoken of Jesus, spoon-feeding him bits of gospel now and then, but never pushing it down his throat. And now Kim, with her pure, sweet faith that Jesus could make him happy.

"And Dawn," he whispered. He still hadn't quite figured out how that pint-sized tornado had swept into his life, but he was glad she had. He didn't know where their relationship was going, or if he was even capable of letting it develop into anything stronger than attraction and budding friendship, but he wanted—needed—to find out.

Dawn's faith ran deep enough to sustain her through a horrible, traumatic period of her life and help her become a joyful, beautiful woman. He knew instinctively that she would never give her heart to a man who didn't share her Christian beliefs. He didn't know if he wanted her love, but he knew he couldn't pretend to believe as she did. Such a faith had to be real. Even if he could fake it for a while, he could not tolerate deception in himself or in another.

"Maybe it's time to really think this through." Grant stood and stretched. "But I've got to get some place more comfortable." He went inside, creeping down the hall to Kim's room and listening to her soft, even breathing. Pushing open the door, he moved silently over to the bed. She was curled up in a ball on her side, a teddy bear cuddled in her arms. Smiling tenderly, he drew the sheet up over her and her friend. As he turned to go, he spotted her Bible on the bedside table and picked it up. Leaving the room, he pulled the door almost closed and walked out to the living room.

He relaxed in his recliner, but there was no danger of him dozing off. Too many thoughts whirled in his mind. For all his bluster, in spite of all the times he had questioned God's existence, in his heart he knew God was real. He supposed he had known it since he was a child. Once he acknowledged that fact, he had no trouble accepting the Bible as God's Word. Another part of his early upbringing, he supposed. "So if there is a God, and the Bible tells us what he wants us to know, then what the Bible says is true."

Grant's mother had given Kim the Bible before she went to camp. He opened it to the first page, noting that his mom had written a Scripture reference, John 3:16, beneath her loving inscription. He found the table of contents and looked up the page number for the book of John. Turning to the verse, he read: "For God so loved the world that he gave his one and only Son, that whoever believes in him shall not perish but have eternal life."

Grant mulled over the words. He knew that Jesus died on the cross. "But why did he have to die?" Frowning, he flipped to the index and checked the listings for the word death. Wade had suggested reading the New Testament, so Grant bounced back and forth between the table of contents and the index for a few minutes to figure out which references were in the New Testament.

He read a couple of verses, but they didn't answer his question. Next he read Romans 4:25, which said, "He was delivered over to death for our sins and was raised to life for our justification." This brought to mind some other things Wade had told him: "Everyone sins, and sin separates us from God. Because God loves us, Jesus died to atone for our sins. He was buried and rose from the grave, just as the Scriptures said he would be."

Grant continued to read in Romans: "Therefore, since we have been justified through faith, we have peace with God through our Lord Jesus Christ.... And we rejoice in the hope of the glory of God."

He suddenly realized that he very much wanted what God was offering him, not just eternal life, but peace and joy. "But how do I get it?" Dawn said salvation was a free gift, but Grant didn't figure anything was free. "What's the catch?"

A tiny sneeze made him look over his shoulder. Kim stood there, sleepily rubbing her nose with one hand and her eye with the other. "What catch?" She yawned. "You're not watchin' football."

Grant set the Bible on the table beside him and held out his arms. She came to him and crawled up in his lap. "What are you doin' awake, punkin?"

She blinked and yawned again, snuggling close with her head on his chest. "I dunno. I woke up and heard you talkin'. Thought somebody was here. Who were you talkin' to?"

"Myself, and I guess to God."

Kim leaned her forearms against his chest and looked up at him. "I didn't know you ever prayed, Daddy."

He adjusted her arms so her elbows wouldn't dig into his stomach. "I guess I used to some when I was a little kid." *But only once as a man.* He had sent a desperate plea toward heaven for the baby-sitter to be wrong—for his wife not to be unfaithful. *Don't reckon even God can change something that's already happened.*

Kim glanced at the table beside his chair, her eyes growing round when she saw her Bible lying there. She sat up in his lap, wide awake. "Were you reading my Bible?"

"A little. I didn't think you'd mind."

"I don't. What were you reading?"

"Some verses about Jesus, about him dying for our sins and being the only way to the Father. And about how much God loves us."

"Cool!"

Grant smiled. "It is pretty awesome." He meant it in the true sense of the word, but Kim rolled her eyes and grinned.

"Daddy, nobody says awesome anymore. That went out a long time ago."

"Oh. Well, let's just say I'm impressed." He put his arm

around his daughter, amazed that they were having this conversation and treasuring it. "But there's something I can't figure out."

She frowned. "What's that?"

"Dawn said salvation is a free gift, and I was just reading that whoever believes in Jesus has eternal life."

She nodded. "That's right."

"But, honey, is that all I have to do? Just believe?"

Kim frowned thoughtfully as she wiggled to a more comfortable position. "Almost. At camp, my counselor said I should thank God for forgiving my sins—it's okay to admit that you sin, 'cause everybody does wrong things even when we try not to. And she said that since eternal life is a gift, we have to accept it, and when we do, Christ will live in our hearts."

Suddenly it all seemed so simple. He didn't have to try to understand it all at once or rationalize everything. He simply had to accept it, the way Kim did. Hadn't Wade even said something about receiving the kingdom of God like a little child? With pure and simple faith.

"Do you want me to pray with you?" asked Kim. "I was a little nervous when I prayed at camp, but Grasshopper—that's my counselor—held my hand. It helped a lot."

Grant nodded. "Yes, honey, I'd like that. I can just talk to him, right? I don't have to say anything special or fancy?"

"Just talk to him, like he was your best friend," she said with a smile. "What's even neater is that you can talk to him anytime, and you don't even need a phone or have to go to his house."

Grant laughed, thankful for his precious little charmer who was making this whole thing easier for him. "Okay, but you'll close your eyes, right? I'd feel funny if you were watchin' me." He felt a little funny anyway, but he wasn't about to turn her away.

She took his big hand in both of her small ones. "I promise I'll close my eyes. Just don't pray too long."

"Yes, ma'am." Grant waited until she closed her eyes, then closed his own. "God, I've messed up a lot in my life. I've done plenty of things wrong." His heart ached with the thought of how much he had done wrong. "Thank you for forgiving my sins and dying for my sins. Thank you for the gift of eternal life. Please live in my heart. Please, Lord, give me the faith to believe and trust in you, not just so I can go to heaven, but so I can be a better man down here on earth." His throat grew thick with emotion, and he prayed silently. *Please give me your peace and joy.* "Thank you, God. Thank you, Jesus."

Grant wasn't sure what he expected—maybe thunder and lightning or a blast of trumpets and a booming voice saying, "It's about time." He waited and tried to listen above the pounding of his heart but heard nothing. Gradually, his pulse slowed and he listened to Kim's soft breathing and a cricket chirping outside the open window. Then he realized God had answered his prayer as a gentle, comforting peace settled over him. The burden of some of his past mistakes did not instantly vanish, but he knew he had someone to help him deal with it.

Opening his eyes, he found Kim peeking at him with one eye open, the other closed.

"You're supposed to say 'in Jesus' name, amen.'"

He followed her directions, then gave her a big bear hug.

"Do you feel better now, Daddy?"

"Yes, punkin, I do."

"Good. Let's go have some cookies and ice cream." Kim scrambled off his lap and headed for the kitchen.

Laughing, Grant followed her, silently thanking God for this beautiful child. Halfway to the kitchen, he realized he had prayed without even thinking about it. The expression of thanks had flowed from a well of gratitude in his heart, and the words had come as easily as if he were talking to a friend. Now he understood what Kim meant when she said talking to God was like talking to her best friend.

Awesome.

Eight

❧

The home-cooked dinner Dawn had promised Grant on Thursday evening turned into a mini welcome-home party for Wade and Andi. The newlyweds had returned to their ranch the evening before, and Dawn couldn't wait to see them. When she had checked with Grant Wednesday night, he assured her he would be glad to have Wade and Andi join them.

While cleaning up the kitchen after the meal, Dawn glanced toward the living room where the men were discussing local politics. The guys had offered to do the dishes while she and Andi put things away, but Dawn had declined. The kitchen wasn't large enough for four people to work, plus she wanted a few minutes to talk to Andi alone.

As if sensing her gaze, Grant looked up, giving her a smile and a wink.

"Well, looks like you two are hitting it off rather well," murmured Andi.

Dawn carried a stack of plates to the sink so Andi could rinse them and put them in the dishwasher. "We are. I've been out at the ranch several times sorting through his aunt's things. If he's around, half the time I wind up wandering down to where he's working and don't get much accomplished."

Andi laughed quietly. "That depends on what you want to accomplish."

Dawn grinned. "He did invite me out last Saturday."

Andi's eyes sparkled. "Where did you go?"

"Nowhere. He hurt his knee that afternoon, and he was really in pain. We ordered pizza and stayed here. Actually, it was very nice," she said with a smug smile. Dawn knew her cousin would pounce on that statement like a duck on a June bug, especially since Dawn had unmercifully grilled Andi after her first real date with Wade.

Andi leaned closer as she lined up the plates in the dishwasher. "Did he kiss you?" she whispered.

"Nosy."

Andi giggled. "A family trait. So? Tell me!" she muttered under her breath.

"Yes, he did. We were out on the porch looking at the stars."

"Are we talkin' fireworks?"

"Let's just say the rings around Saturn are quite lovely close up, but he was also very sweet and a gentleman," said Dawn, taking a small plastic container out of the cabinet to hold the leftover stroganoff. "Actually, I think that kiss scared him, but not enough to send him packin'."

"That's good. Uh-oh, here they come." Andi poured dishwasher soap into the holder and shut the door as Wade and Grant strolled into the kitchen.

"Are you slaves, er, ladies finished in here?" Wade asked, stepping up behind his wife and slipping his arms around her.

"We're done." When Andi looked up at him over her shoulder, he kissed her cheek.

"Then let's go outside and count the stars." Wade propelled Andi toward the backyard. Grinning, he looked back at Grant and Dawn. "Y'all can tag along, if you want."

"We'll be along directly," said Grant, leaning against the kitchen counter. After they went out the door, he smiled. "Do you think they'll notice that it's not even dark yet?"

"Probably not."

"It's good to see them so happy." Grant slid his arm around Dawn's waist. "That was a great dinner."

"Thanks. Wait until you taste my special dessert."

"What is it?" he asked, shifting a little closer.

"I call it BPM."

He thought for a minute. "Banana peanut munchies?"

She laughed, shaking her head. "Baked peach mixture. I found the recipe in the paper several years ago. They didn't have a name for it, just said it was a tasty baked peach mixture, so I christened it BPM. It tastes like the gooey part of peach cobbler. It's wonderful with gobs of whipped cream."

"Sounds good, but how do you stay so slim eatin' like this? Rich stroganoff, whipped cream, that wonderful homemade bread."

"Fast metabolism. I'm hyper, remember?"

"Only part of the time. Reckon you just keep busy. Which reminds me of something else I was wondering about. When did you find time to make bread?"

"Hey, bucko, I may be old-fashioned in some ways, but in others I'm a nineties woman—I have an automatic bread machine. Dump in the ingredients, turn that little sucker on, and four hours later you take out a perfect loaf of homemade bread. It mixes the dough, let's it rise, and cooks it. Even you could do it."

He lifted an eyebrow and drew her around in front of him, settling his hands at her waist. "Even me, huh? I'll have you know, I'm not a bad cook."

"Oh?" She pretended to straighten the collar of his turquoise and purple Western shirt. She loved the geometric patterns that reminded her of an Indian blanket. "Then how come all you ever have is sandwich fixin's or frozen dinners when I'm out there?"

"I can cook. I just don't. Don't have time. Besides, it's too big a hassle to cook for one person. I manage decent meals when Kim's around." He wrinkled his brow. "Well, sometimes I do. She'd eat macaroni and cheese every night if I'd let her."

"Good stuff. And easy." Dawn reached down beside him and opened a lower cabinet door. Six boxes of macaroni and cheese sat on the shelf, along with various other pasta mixes. "Greene's has it on sale, four for a dollar, but this is the last week. Better get over there."

He laughed and pushed the cabinet door closed. "And you only bought six?"

"Ate two already." Dawn smiled, enjoying their banter and being with him. Looking into his bright blue eyes, she watched in fascination as their color darkened, reminding her of a sapphire pendant on display at Memory Lane.

He leaned toward her slightly and inhaled. "Flowers tonight?" When she nodded, he smiled. "You always smell so good.

"So do you."

102

He laughed ruefully. "Not always."

"Unless you've been hanging onto a horse too long," she amended. "But even if you've been working, I can still smell your aftershave—sometimes tangy, sometimes spicy. I like both kinds."

"That's good, because I don't buy anything expensive."

She smiled and toyed with his collar again. "You could probably wear horse liniment and I'd like it."

"I doubt it, and I know I wouldn't." He caressed her cheek with his thumb, his fingers sifting through her hair. "Have I told you how much I like your smile?"

"No, but you can tell me now."

"It's like a brilliant ray of sunshine breaking through an overcast sky, warming me right here." He laid his fingers lightly over his heart.

"Oh, Grant, how sweet." She skidded about a mile farther down the road toward love.

He laughed softly. "Surprised you, didn't I? We'd better get on outside before they come looking for us."

"They've probably forgotten we're even here."

When they walked out onto the porch, Wade and Andi were sprawled in the grass arguing about the location of the big dipper. "It will be right up there," insisted Andi pointing straight up.

"Nope." Wade tickled her nose with a blade of grass. "It'll be over that way." He pointed toward the north.

"You said the other direction a minute ago." She crossed her arms in obviously faked indignation.

"Are you two having a spat?" Grant eased down on the porch,

resting his feet on the steps, and caught Dawn's hand, guiding her down next to him.

"Just enough of one so we can kiss and make up," Wade said, grinning wolfishly.

"He's incorrigible."

"Aw, darlin', you love tryin' to reform me, and you know it."

Dawn looked at Grant. "We might as well go back inside. They're not going to tell us about Grand Cayman Island anyway."

Andi sat up. "Oh, yes, we will. It's absolutely beautiful! Warm—"

"Hot!" said Wade.

"Hot—with lovely white sand beaches. Even though there were lots of tourists, it didn't seem crowded at the beach. When we went snorkeling and skin diving, we saw all kinds and colors of fish. Fluorescent and iridescent blue, green, red, yellow. You name it. There's a parrot fish that changes colors depending on your angle."

"When we went skin diving, the sting rays would swim by and rub up against our legs," said Wade.

"Isn't that dangerous?"

"Not if you avoid the sharp hook on their tails. They can really hurt you if they want to, but it seemed as if they only wanted to play. Guess they're used to people. We shot three rolls of film underwater. We'll show you the pictures and slides next time you're out at the Smoking Pipe."

Dawn rolled her eyes. "Uh-oh, the old 'come over and we'll show you pictures of our vacation' routine."

"Could be worse," said Grant. "They might have gone to the

Sahara. Sand dunes instead of fish."

They chatted for a while about the island, their trip to Disneyworld, and their time in Nashville. Andi asked Dawn how the museum project was coming, so she filled them in on some of their planned displays.

"We're going to have a big section devoted to ranching, with pictures and paraphernalia from about 1880 up through the thirties or forties. We had quite a number of things in the old museum we can use for the exhibit, and people have loaned or given us other things."

Wade's aunt and uncle had been very generous. "Ray and Della gave us some of her grandfather's things—a saddle, chaps, saddle bags, and a worn-out pair of boots. Others have donated ropes, spurs, bridles, branding irons, odds and ends." She sighed wistfully. "If I could find an old chuck wagon, I'd be happy as a pig in slop."

Grant laughed, sliding his arm around her. "That's all it takes, huh?"

She glanced up at him, then pulled back slightly to look at him more closely. She had seen that mischievous anticipation in his eyes another time—right before she first opened the door to the bunkhouse. "You have one?"

He grinned.

"Where? Grant Adams, do you have an old chuck wagon stashed some place?"

"I don't reckon I've shown you the barn yet, have I, sugar?" he drawled.

"You know very well you haven't shown me the barn." She gave him a pointed look. "What's out there?"

"Some hay and about twenty sacks of feed. 'Course all that's in the granary on one side. There are saddles and bridles and horse stuff in the tack room."

"The wagon, Grant. Where is it?"

"You mean the buckboard, the buggy, or the chuck wagon?" He might have pulled off the innocent expression if imps hadn't been dancing in his eyes.

Dawn stared at him. Finally, she whispered, "You have all three?"

He smiled gently. "Yep. They're in pretty good shape, too. Want to borrow them?"

She threw her arms around his neck and kissed him, then promptly forgot about the museum and horse-drawn vehicles when he took advantage of the opportunity and kissed her back. When he slowly raised his head, it took her a moment to remember where they were and who else was there. Heat rushed to her face when she glanced at Wade and Andi. "All right, you two, quit grinnin'."

"Yes, ma'am," said Wade, his smile growing even wider.

Dawn decided to ignore them and looked up at Grant. "Why didn't you tell me about them?"

He shrugged. "I was going to. Just hadn't gotten around to it."

She smiled. "I have a 'round to it' in the kitchen. Maybe I should give it to you."

"Naw, then I'd have to catch up on everything." His expression grew serious. "I'd be happy to loan the buggy and wagons to the museum, but I don't want to get rid of them permanently. They were my great-granddaddy's pride and joy. When Mr.

Ainsworth bought the ranch from Dad, I asked him to hang onto them for me. He promised he would, and he kept his word. The first section of land I bought was the one with the house and outbuildings on it, because I wanted to make sure those vehicles didn't disappear."

"We'll take very good care of them."

"I know you will," he said, confident his treasured possessions were in good hands.

When they went inside for dessert, Wade and Andi sat in the two chairs in the living room, leaving the couch for Grant and Dawn. After Grant complimented Dawn on the baked peach mixture, he casually asked if anyone knew of a place in town where a man could buy a Bible.

"They have some at the drugstore," said Wade, slowly setting his spoon back into his bowl of dessert and watching Grant closely.

Out of the corner of his eye, Grant noticed that Dawn started to take a bite, then set the spoon down, too. Andi glanced at Wade, then focused her gaze on Grant.

"You askin' for yourself or somebody else?" Wade asked.

"For myself." Grant suddenly felt shy and a little embarrassed. As if sensing his uncertainty, Dawn reached over and wrapped her hand around his. He gripped it tightly. "I figure when a man's accepted Jesus, he ought to spend some time readin' up on how he's supposed to live."

He felt Dawn hug his arm and rest her head on his shoulder, but he couldn't look away from Wade. As his old friend slowly set the bowl on the coffee table, his expression was a mixture of joy and raw emotion. Wade met his gaze, and Grant saw moisture in his eyes. A big lump lodged in his throat.

"When?" asked Wade quietly, his voice thick.

"Monday evening." After clearing his throat, Grant told them about hearing Kim say her prayers and the other things that had happened. "When I started talkin' to God, I guess I was a little louder than I meant to be because Kim woke up and came out to see who was there.

"I surprised myself by admitting what I was doing. She's quite the kid. Before I knew it, we were having a theological discussion." He heard Dawn sniff, so he shifted his weight and pulled his handkerchief out of his back pocket, handing it to her. She mumbled her thanks, wiped her eyes, and blew her nose, all the while keeping her arm looped around his. When he saw Wade wipe his eyes on the heel of his hand, and Andi hop up to retrieve a box of tissues from the kitchen window, he almost had to ask Dawn for his handkerchief back.

He cleared his throat again as Andi plopped down on the chair, jerking tissues out of the box for herself and Wade. "Anyway, she clarified a couple of things for me and explained how she had prayed to receive Christ at camp. Then she took my hand and gave me courage while I asked him to live in my heart." He smiled. "Then we had cookies and ice cream."

Wade stood and reached over the coffee table to shake Grant's hand, then pulled him off the couch and gave him an enthusiastic hug. "Welcome to the family, brother."

"Thanks."

Andi gave him a hug, too. "You'll find being in God's hands a very nice place," she said with a warm smile. "I know because I walked without him for a long time."

As Wade and Andi went back to their chairs, Grant sat down and looked at Dawn. Tears trailed down her cheeks and across the edges of her sweet, beautiful smile.

"I'm so happy for you," she whispered.

He gathered her in his embrace and held her tightly.

After a few minutes, she pulled away, dabbing at the wet spot on his shirt with the handkerchief. "Sorry I got your shirt wet."

"It'll dry, and I won't melt."

"Will you come to church with us on Sunday?" asked Wade. "You could stop by the house and ride in with us."

"I'll come, but I'll drive myself." He smiled. "In case I decide to bolt like a jack rabbit."

Wade laughed. "I don't think you'll feel the need for speed. We're pretty laid back."

"Do I have to get all gussied up?" Grant practically shuddered at the thought of wearing a suit, then remembered that he didn't have one. He'd thrown it out with relish when he and Susan split up.

"No. Some men wear them and some don't. Jeans are okay."

Grant breathed a sigh of relief. "That's good. Otherwise, I'd have to do some fast shopping."

The mantel clock whirred and clanged a tinny chime ten times. Wade chuckled and tossed a pillow at Dawn. "You ever gonna get a clock that doesn't sound like a hammer hittin' a can?"

"Nope. That one belonged to Granny Mae. I like it just fine, thank you."

Wade looked at Andi and smiled. "It's past our bedtime." He stood and pulled Andi out of the chair. "Come on, woman. Time to hit the trail."

"Yes, master," she said dryly, winking at Dawn. "Sounds real tough, doesn't he?"

"Big, bad, and ugly," Dawn said, giggling when Wade pretended to be offended. "It's good to have y'all home. Come back again now that you know where I live."

Grant and Dawn walked out with them, waiting until Wade pulled his bright red roadster away from the curb before returning inside.

"Guess I'd better be going, too." *But I don't want to.*

"Do you have a few minutes? I have some of Aunt Lena's things ready to take to the store, but I want your final approval. You might see something else you want to keep."

"Sure, I can hang around a little while." He tried not to sound too eager. He followed her to the garage, where she had several long tables set up with dozens of items arranged according to type. He carefully looked through them, setting aside a knife and a shaving mug he recognized as his great-grandfather's.

He was amazed at the prices on some of the items. A 1910 calendar with a picture of a lady on it advertising De Laval Cream Separators was priced at three hundred fifty dollars, and a program from the St Louis vs. Yankees 1926 World Series had a price tag of five hundred dollars. Stopping at an assortment of glass candy containers made in the shape of comic characters, animals, and household appliances, he smiled, remembering that Aunt Lena always had one or another of them filled with hard candy.

He picked up one that looked like an old-fashioned refrigerator but almost dropped it when he saw the price tag. Dawn breathed a sigh of relief as he glanced up.

"Whew! I thought that one was going to bite the concrete," she said, leaning dramatically against the side of the table.

"Is this the right price? Can this thing be worth thirteen hundred dollars?"

"Yes. I even called Alex, my friend in Fort Worth, to verify it. I won't put that in any of the stores out here. We'll need to give it to him to sell on consignment, along with several other things. We won't make as much because of his commission, but I'm sure we'll get the money faster because things will sell quicker. They could sit here for years before a buyer happened through. The candy containers vary a great deal in value, ranging from about fifty dollars on up. Bless your aunt for loving candy and for taking such good care of these. At the risk of giving you a heart attack, that one of Jackie Coogan should bring about twelve hundred dollars."

"I think I'd better leave before I pass out." It boggled Grant's mind to consider what else might still be sitting in the boxes out at the ranch. Dawn had only gone through half of them. He spotted four kerosene lamps on the table. "I wouldn't mind having one of those lamps. Could come in handy during a thunderstorm."

"Take your pick."

He took a lamp, the knife, and shaving cup and walked back into the living room, setting them on an end table. Dawn followed, handing him a small pair of pearl-handled scissors. "I had these set aside. Are they the ones you wanted?"

As Grant took the scissors, memories swept through his mind. "They're the ones. Aunt Lena kept them in her crochet bag to cut thread, but she wasn't above using them to take a tag out of a boy's shirt if it was buggin' him." He set them with the other things. "Thanks."

Dawn had brought Kim into town for a while Monday afternoon to see if there was anything she wanted. She took home the teddy bear she'd been sleeping with that night and a little black woolly lamb. Dawn explained that she didn't think they were particularly valuable. It wouldn't have mattered to him if they were. If Kim wanted them she could have them. If they'd been valuable, however, he might have encouraged her not to sleep with them. "Did Kim find anything else she wanted?"

"Some tin Cracker Jack prizes. They range in value from thirty to a hundred dollars."

"When I think of all those prizes I threw away…"

She laughed. "We all moan about that. Of course, if everybody had saved them, they wouldn't be worth anything. She did find a beautiful cut glass vase that she fell in love with. It's valuable, but it would be a wonderful addition to her hope chest."

"Don't even think about a hope chest. She's only ten."

"I've been collecting things for my hope chest since I was eight. Of course, most things never get to the chest; I have them sitting all over the house or am using them in one way or another."

"All right. She can have them, but let's just say it's for when she's grown. I don't want to even think about her dating, much less gettin' married."

He rested his hand on her shoulder. "How about spending the day with me on Saturday. Kim will be at her friend Jenny's all weekend, then they head off to camp Sunday afternoon. So it would be just you, me, and about twenty or thirty others, not counting horses."

She laughed. "Do you usually count the horses?"

"They're good company; sometimes better than the two-legged kind."

"I suppose that's true. Are you going to a cutting competition?"

"Just a practice one. There is usually an event of some kind going on most weekends. Some pay money. Some don't. It's good for the horses to stay used to being around a group of people and other animals. This one is at the Double L Ranch northeast of Sidell. It's liable to be hot and dusty with varying levels of entertainment, but I can promise you a good steak dinner. Pete and Marla usually put on quite a feast at the ranch."

"I don't know." She frowned thoughtfully.

Grant's good spirits plummeted. She'd seemed to enjoy watching him work with Dancer, but he supposed that was just a put-on. Cutting was a big part of his life, and he'd hoped she would take an interest in it. *Maybe I shouldn't have mentioned the hot and dusty part.* "If you'd rather not, I understand," he said, barely able to keep the disappointment out of his voice.

"I'd like to go," she said quickly. "I think it would be fun, but I'm not sure if Emily can handle the store by herself on a Saturday. She's worked alone some during the week and has helped on Saturdays, but I've never left her alone when it was busy. Actually, I'm not even sure if she can work then. May I think about it and see how she feels and give you a call tomorrow?"

"Sure." He'd been hoping so much she'd jump at the chance that he hadn't even thought about her store. "If it doesn't work out, maybe we can get together Sunday afternoon."

"Sorry. I can't. I'm helping with a ninetieth birthday party for one of the ladies at church. You could come if you wanted, but I've got kitchen duty."

"No, thanks. I'd feel strange going to a party for somebody I don't even know."

"At least I'll see you at church Sunday. That'll be nice."

"I was hoping you'd go with me." He was counting on it. Otherwise, he was afraid he might get cold feet.

"I'd love to. It's been a while since a handsome man gave me a ride to church. Just remember who you're with when all the single women start making a fuss over you."

"You make it sound as if I'll get mobbed."

"You might. You'll be the best looking man to wander through those door lately."

He searched her eyes, warmed by the approval he saw there. "You're mighty good at boostin' a man's ego," he said softly, putting his arms around her.

"And don't you forget it." She smiled and leaned slightly toward him. "I don't think I've been particularly good at that before. Guess I've been shy about speaking my mind."

He chuckled and took a tiny step closer. "I can't imagine you being shy or not speaking your mind."

"I have my moments."

"Is this one of them?"

"It's probably a good time to keep my thoughts to myself," she murmured.

He cradled her face in his hand and watched her eyelids slowly drift closed. "Then I think I'll hire out at the carnival." When she looked at him, he smiled. "I'd do a fantastic job as a mind reader."

"Only with me."

As the truth of her whispered words echoed through his mind, he pulled her into a tight embrace, kissing her slowly, lingering in her sweetness. Straightening, he reluctantly released her. "I'd better git. Mornin' comes early." He took a few steps to the coat rack by the door where he'd left his hat. "It'll be early on Saturday, too."

"What time?"

"Seven," he mumbled, putting on his hat.

"Excuse me? I didn't quite get that." She stepped up beside him, one eyebrow arched loftily. "I only know of two times that start with an 's', and I'm not real excited about either one of them."

"Well, see," he said with a bright smile, "it could be worse. I could have said six."

"Seven! You actually expect me to be ready to go on a date at seven on a Saturday morning? You've been out in the sun too long, Adams."

"That's why we start early, so we won't work the horses too hard when it's hot. Normally, I would have left a little earlier." He nudged her chin up with his finger. "You don't have to be wide awake. Just dressed and able to walk to the truck. I'll even carry you. All you'd have to do is hang on to the thermos of coffee."

"We'll see." She crossed her arms, then tipped her head. "Only if you bring donuts. Chocolate-covered ones."

"Dawn, I'll buy you every chocolate donut in the bakery at Greene's if you'll go with me."

"I'll talk to Emily. If she's willing to work by herself, I'll let her. I think she'll do fine. And I don't need every donut. Just six."

"You'll make yourself sick."

"It's going to be a long day. I'll need sustenance."

"I'll bring sandwiches." He lightly tapped the end of her nose.

"We'll need those, too. If you're nice, I'll share my donuts."

"I'll be very nice." He dropped a kiss on her forehead. "But Dancer can't have any, no matter how hard he begs."

Nine

❧

On Saturday morning, Dawn cradled a half-full cup of coffee in her hands and stared blurry-eyed at the passing scenery as they drove toward the Double L Ranch. Hearing a soft chuckle, she lazily turned her head toward Grant. "See somethin' funny, cowboy?"

"No, ma'am," he said, with a twinkle in his eyes. "Just a cute zombie. I didn't really believe you when you said it took a while to get goin' in the mornings."

"Corrected that misconception, haven't we?" She hid a yawn behind one hand. "I think I'm doing rather well. I haven't spilled the coffee yet, even if you've hit every pothole in the road."

He laughed. "There aren't any potholes on the highway. I admit I could use some new shocks for this ol' pickup. It's not used to carrying pretty ladies. Plumb forgot how to cushion the ride."

"Maybe I'll trade places with Dancer or Gus." She glanced in the outside mirror at the horse trailer. "They don't seem to be bouncing too much."

"No way, Gus hogs the seat, and Dancer tries to drive."

She laughed and took another sip of coffee. The morning was beautiful with one tiny cloud drifting across the clear blue sky. She could understand why the riders would want to start early and enjoy the peaceful coolness. "Want a doughnut?"

"Sure. I wouldn't mind a drink of that coffee, either."

She handed him the cup and took two doughnuts from the cardboard box from the bakery. Setting one pastry on a napkin on her lap, she traded him a chocolate-covered doughnut for the now empty coffee cup. "Thirsty, huh?" After pouring herself more coffee from the thermos, she relaxed and ate her breakfast, noting the scenery had changed to steep-sided hills and deep canyons. "This is pretty country. I don't think I've ever been up this way. I didn't realize it was so rugged."

"Pure ranch country. Not good for anything else, except maybe a few oil wells. Takes a lot of land per cow up through here. I admire the scenery, but I wouldn't want to try to make a livin' off of it."

"Your land is strictly cattle country, too, isn't it? I didn't see any crops."

"I have a couple of fields where I raise Sudan and wheat, but it's mostly range land. Cotton sure won't grow there. Daddy tried it, and that's part of why we went belly-up. I prefer critters to plants anyway. At least with cows, you can buy feed if there's no grass."

"If you can afford it. From what I hear, feed is expensive."

"It is. A man can go broke real fast if he's not careful. I buy hay from Wade and supplement with it when I need to. He has better farm land than I do. I'm doin' all right, though. Don't owe anybody anything. I learned that lesson when Daddy lost the ranch.

"He kept borrowing from the bank, figuring that all he needed was one good year to straighten everything out. Unfortunately, we had several dry years in a row, and a couple of those he'd tried to expand into cotton farming. Finally, he had more bills than he could ever pay, and the bank foreclosed. Our neighbor, Mr. Ainsworth, bought it right away and promised me that I could buy it back if I was ever in a position to do it."

"And you've been working toward that goal ever since. It's an admirable dream, Grant. I hope it comes true." Dawn wiped her fingers on a napkin and screwed the coffee cup on the thermos. When she looked up he was studying her closely.

"Hey, cowboy, you're supposed to watch the road, not me."

"You're nicer to look at."

"Thanks a heap. I'd better be." She stretched and smiled at him. "Good morning."

"Good morning." He smiled lazily. "So you're finally awake?"

"All charged up and full of pep."

"Don't get too rambunctious. You won't be doin' much but sitting all day."

"Better that than trying to stay on a horse, especially one that's jumping all over the place."

"You'll have to try it sometime, after you learn to ride, of course. Kim's horse is a cutter, and she's learning. It won't be long before she can compete in the youth division if she wants to."

"So this is not just a macho male sport?"

"Nope. Some of the best riders are of the female variety. Put 'em on a good cuttin' horse, and they have as good a shot at winning. I guess one of the things I like about cutting is that it isn't predictable. There are some folks who win consistently, but not always the top prize. And, on rare occasions, they're knocked out of the money completely. Sometimes a nobody like me takes home some of the bacon. The rider has to know what he or she is doing, the horse has to know what's goin' on and love doin' it, but in the end, the cow plays a big roll in determining the winner. If you cut a cow that won't move or just runs off, then there's no way to win."

Dawn propped one boot up on the dash. Given the dusty disarray of the inside of the truck, she didn't think he'd mind. "Is there some way to judge how a cow will do? When we watched you work the other day, you seemed very definite about which calf you wanted to cut."

"I've learned some tricks. That's one thing about cuttin', folks are quick to share their knowledge and experience. At the competitions, the herd holders will help you pick a cow that hasn't been worked. I try to keep a close eye on the group so I know which ones have done their duty. They'll be tired and not show as well.

"You watch how the others respond when a rider goes into the herd to make a cut. You want one that acknowledges the horse but doesn't overreact by running around and acting wild. The good ones will move slower than the others, and when they're out in front of the herd, they don't make a mad dash back to hide in the herd. The English breeds, like Hereford, Angus, or black-baldies which are a Hereford-Angus mix, are gentle. They'll give you more time to show the horse. Brahmas or Brahma crosses are fast and can be real difficult to handle. Wilder cattle are more of a challenge, but it's also easier to make mistakes.

"I guess a lot of it comes from experience. You don't want a cow that's too wild, but you need one with enough gumption to help show off your horse. You sure don't want one that's listless or stupid." He chuckled. "And believe me, there are some stupid cows. I watch for the ones with bright eyes—and make sure they have two good eyes. Every so often, a calf that is blind in one eye accidentally gets overlooked in the first sort. If the critter can't see, he's liable to run right into you."

"Poor thing."

"Yeah, I always feel kinda sorry for them, too. They must be scared out of their wits." He turned off the highway onto a gravel drive. Two tall thick posts stood on each side of the road, supporting a huge log, forming the entrance to the Double L Ranch.

As they passed beneath it, Dawn turned in the seat and looked out the back window. "That's no mesquite tree sittin' up there."

"Fir. He had it shipped all the way from the state of Washington. Has a cousin up that way who runs a loggin' company. He wanted something impressive."

"He got it." She turned back around in the seat. "Are cutting horses specially bred like race horses?"

"As a rule, yes. Occasionally one comes along that's an exception, like Dancer, a regular ol' horse with nothing distinguishing about his family at all."

She watched as his face softened with an affectionate yet bemused smile. "Where did you find him?"

"I was coming home from San Angelo one afternoon a couple of years ago and passed a place with a 'for sale' sign hanging on the gate. The homeliest, skinniest horse I'd ever seen was standin' by the fence lookin' plumb pitiful. He was in terrible shape but not beyond saving. I stopped and walked over to the fence, and he came right up to me. He was alert even though he shouldn't have been. His eyes glowed with intelligence and heart, and he had me pegged as a sucker the minute he saw me. I could practically hear him asking me to take him home, that he'd be a good horse and earn his keep.

"I bought him on the spot. He'd never been ridden, but he wasn't skittish around people. I had to go home for my trailer, and when I picked him up, he actually looked happy. He came trottin' up to meet me like he had been afraid I wasn't going to come back for him. I think he knew I was the last chance he had."

"If this story doesn't lighten up, you're going to lose your handkerchief again," said Dawn, blinking hard against the stinging in her eyes.

He smiled. "Don't you ever carry a Kleenex?"

"I've probably got one wadded up in the bottom of my purse. Believe me, it would be easier to borrow your handkerchief."

"I'll quit with the sob story. I took him home and had the vet take a look at him. Fed him a few dozen bottles of pills and elixir and a ton of feed. Anything the vet thought would help."

"And love."

"That, too. After a while, he started feelin' frisky. One day I saw him playin' with a butterfly."

"You've got to be kidding."

Grant shook his head, a grin lighting up his face. "A butterfly. That crazy horse was dartin' here and there, stalking the thing. And every time he came to a stop, he'd crouch down like he was darin' that flutterby to try to get away from him. I'd been to some cutting events strictly as a spectator, but he sure looked like he had the makin's of a cuttin' horse to me."

122

"So you broke him and started training him?"

"Something like that. I asked Pete Davis to come over and take a look at him. You'll meet Pete today. He owns the Double L. He's been into cutting for most of his life. Took one look at Dancer and gave him his stamp of approval, only he said a horse that danced that purty ought to be called something better than Brownie."

"I agree. Dancer seems fitting."

"It is. I broke him and studied up on training him. Then we both spent some time with Pete, who's also a professional trainer. I couldn't afford to have Pete do all the training, but he was kind enough to teach me so I could do most of the work."

"Sounds like it paid off at the Futurity."

"Yes, ma'am. Hopefully, it will pay off at the Derby, too. I could put that money to good use."

"Buying more land?"

He glanced at her, his expression guarded, yet determined. "I've got a ways to go, but some day I'm going to own all seven thousand acres."

"I hope you do."

He studied her face, then turned his attention back to the road. A tiny frown creased his brow. "Do you really mean that, or are you just saying it because you think I want to hear it?"

"I mean it. I'm the history buff, remember? I know how important it can be to hold onto what families acquired through their work and sacrifice. Roots run deep, especially when it comes to ranches and farms. There is something about owning land that's intrinsic with freedom." She frowned. "Why did you think I didn't mean it?"

He shrugged. "When I first met Susan—my wife—she seemed to agree with my goal of getting the ranch back. But after we got married and she realized that it meant sacrifice, it suddenly became a foolish dream. She hated the ranch and took every opportunity to tell me about it. I know I should have spent more money on her, given her more of the things she wanted, but it seemed a waste at the time."

"What kind of things?" asked Dawn, thinking of his house. Maybe if he'd fixed it up or built Susan a new one, she might not have been so unhappy. Personally, she thought it could be a very warm and charming home with the right touches and some new kitchen appliances. His mother must have bought the stove in the fifties.

"An expensive house in Dallas, designer clothes, diamonds, trips to high-class resorts. I met her at a rodeo, but she was from a wealthy family and was used to that sort of thing. At first she said it didn't matter...."

Dawn waited, giving him time to gather his thoughts, not wanting to prompt him into saying anything he might regret.

His sigh seemed to come from the depths of his soul. "And maybe it wouldn't have mattered so much if I'd been there for her. Being on the rodeo circuit doesn't leave much time for family life, but that was the fastest way I could see to earning the kind of money I needed."

She had no words of comfort for him, but silently prayed that God would ease the burdens on his heart. "Unfortunately, we can usually see things more clearly after the fact. All I know is how much I love my grandmother's house. Losing it would be like tearing out my heart. I'd try to move heaven and earth to get it back."

"Then you understand." He drove by the ranch house and past the barns and regular corrals to a larger pen. "This is the same size as the one at Will Rogers Coliseum in Fort Worth where the big events are held. Pete figures it helps the horses get a feel for the place. In fact, it's almost a replica of the arena. About the only thing missin' is real grandstands."

Dawn looked around at the dozen pickups and horse trailers parked near the pen. "Do you just sit on the ground?"

"Usually I sit on the front of the pickup, but you'll probably be more comfortable on the hay." He pointed to some makeshift bleachers made of stacked hay bales on the other side and stopped the pickup. "They're not bad, and they don't get as hot as the hood of the truck, either."

"Hay it is. I'm glad I borrowed one of Andi's hats. I brought sunscreen, but I'd still be cooked before lunch." She plucked the wide-brimmed straw cowboy hat from between them on the seat and put it on. "What do you think?"

He unfastened his seat belt and leaned toward her. "Purtiest cowgirl I ever did see." Tugging the brim down a tiny bit farther on her forehead, he added, "You're going to be a major distraction."

"I thought you were supposed to let Dancer do all the work anyway."

"I do my share. I get to pick out the cow and hang on."

"If you fall off and Dancer keeps working the cow, can he win?"

"No. There's a legend about a horse doing exactly that, but now you get an automatic sixty from each judge, the lowest score." A gleam of excitement sparkled in his eyes. "Shall we unload?"

"You unload. I'll watch and bring along the food." She almost laughed as his gaze drifted to the other entrants. *Already sizing up the competition.* "And Grant…"

"Yes?" he said, obviously distracted by a rider and horse about to go inside the pen.

"I know it'll be hard, but try to have a good time."

He looked back at her, his expression mildly sheepish. "Honey, I know I'll enjoy today. I just hope you do."

"Horses, cows, sun, dust, the choice between prickly hay or the hot seat." Impulsively, she leaned forward and kissed his cheek. "And handsome cowboys. What more can a gal ask for? It'll be a blast."

Ten

The day started out well, with Grant and Dancer making almost the highest score possible in the first go-round. Pleased with his ride and assured of going on to the next level, Grant dismounted and led Dancer to the warm-up pen where he tied him with the other horses. He patted his neck and heaped praise on him.

As Grant walked toward the gate, he glanced in Dawn's direction, hoping to see her smiling at him. She was engrossed in watching the next rider and getting a step-by-step account of the run from a cowboy sitting in the spot Grant had vacated when he left for his ride. Quick hot anger poured through him as the man leaned close to Dawn's ear to be heard above the calls of the crowd. She didn't seem to mind the man's proximity; in fact, she moved her head a little nearer as the noise increased.

Grant shoved open the gate, startling a nearby horse. He shut the gate, taking his time with the latch in an effort to calm down. Sheltered by the fence, he watched her. The run was over, and she clapped and smiled along with the rest of the crowd. Pete's wife, Marla, sat in front of her, but there were men on every other side. All men he knew. Some he had considered his friends. He tried to be rational—after all, there were only a handful of women present—but as he scanned the crowd, he didn't see any of them surrounded by men making fools of themselves.

Just like Susan. Bitter memories flashed across Grant's mind like flickering film from an old movie. At rodeos or parties, his wife had always been surrounded by men. He had ignored her flirting, considering it merely a part of her vibrant, outgoing personality. In a way, he was even flattered because other men found her alluring. And proud, oh, so proud that she was his. Or so he thought. After they separated, he heard rumors that there had been other men throughout their marriage, but he couldn't accept it. She had always made him believe he was the only one right up until he saw the truth with his own eyes.

Grant pulled his thoughts from the past and focused on Dawn as she talked to Marla. When the cowboy behind her leaned forward and said something, she looked up at him and smiled that saucy smile of hers, apparently coming back with some clever retort because everyone around her laughed. *It'll be a blast.* "If this keeps up, I'm gonna blast somebody clear over to the next county."

Walking toward her, Grant tamped his anger, somewhat reassured when she nudged one of the men next to her to scoot over so he could sit down. When he eased down on the hay, realizing for the first time that his knee ached, she slipped her hand around his and squeezed.

"You were wonderful!"

As he gazed at the admiration shining in her eyes, his anger settled into disquieting uncertainty. "Enjoyed it, did you?"

"I was so excited I couldn't make up my mind whether to

hold my breath or scream."

"So she did both," the man on the other side of her said with a laugh. "I had to tell her to breathe, and when she did, she started hollerin' like crazy."

How did he know she wasn't breathing? Looking over the top of her curls at his used-to-be-friend, he asked quietly, "Clare couldn't make it today?"

The man shook his head, acting as if he had no idea of his transgression. "Like I was tellin' Dawn, she took the twins and the rest of her Girl Scout troop off to camp. I'm batchin' this week."

"Actin' like it, too," muttered Grant, ignoring the man's startled expression.

"Hey, Grant." The man behind him nudged his back with the toe of his boot. "Where'd a no-account hombre like you find such a pretty little filly?"

"None of your business." Grant pulled his hand loose from Dawn's and possessively slid his arm around her waist as several of the men laughed. "Havin' fun?"

"Yes." She smiled up at him. "Except you rode too early. I didn't know enough to realize you'd done so well until the guy over there told me you almost made a perfect score."

"And you were still holdin' your breath and screaming?"

"It looked fantastic to me, even in my ignorance." She leaned closer and whispered, "It looked a whole lot harder and better done than the two runs ahead of you."

Relaxing, he chuckled. "It was, and the scores indicate it."

"I wasn't paying that much attention to the scoring, so I didn't have any idea how they had done."

He wondered what she had been doing. "I guess the guys were busy bending your ear."

"No. Well, yes, but I wasn't paying much attention to them, either."

He looked down at her, surprised to see her face turn pink. "What were you doing?"

"Eating another doughnut and digging one out for Marla. We were talkin', too."

Another rider entered the arena and began to move silently through the herd. Although Grant felt she was being evasive, he decided not to push it. The woman in the arena was probably his closest competition at the event, and he needed to see how she worked.

Dawn watched silently, gasping now and then as the little mare made a quick turn or skidding halt. When the ride was over, she looked up at Grant, her eyes wide. "They're really good."

"Yes, they are, and they're in top form today."

"You and Dancer can beat them, though, can't you?"

"Maybe. Depends on the final go-round." He grimaced as the scores were posted. "We're tied, so it'll be tough."

They spent the next couple of hours watching the competition and enjoying each other's company. At least he thought she enjoyed being with him. She certainly didn't snub the people around them, and even though he didn't really want her to offend anyone, he couldn't stop the jab of jealousy every time she smiled at another man or laughed at someone's joke.

Then he had to leave her to tend to Dancer and ride in the next go-round. He didn't do as well as the first time but still scored fairly high. He made the mistake of looking up at her after his run. Though she was clapping, once again, she was listening intently to the man beside her—a different man this time. His temper rising, he watched as the man behind her left and two others practically fought over the spot.

Taking a turn as herd holder came next. It was difficult to keep his mind on the job at hand, but he managed it. Barely. When he went back to the haystack bleachers, she was involved in an animated discussion with a handsome, young cowboy and seemed not to notice his arrival. The man glanced arrogantly at Grant, clearly indicating that he intended to stay right where he was and that if he had his way, he'd be the one driving her home.

Grant saw red. "Boy, if you know what's good for you, you'll move right now." He doubled up his fists, waiting—even hoping—the man would meet his challenge. Maybe that would ease the rage roiling inside of him.

Dawn stopped in mid-sentence and looked at Grant, her eyes growing wide and the color draining from her face. "Grant? What's wrong?"

"Stay out of this, Dawn. This is between me and junior."

The young man shot to his feet. "You think you can take me? A washed up ol' rodeo bum like you?"

"Stop it! Both of you!" cried Dawn.

"Go ahead," taunted the cowboy.

"Grant, calm down! Please, don't do this!" begged Dawn.

He didn't dare look away from the other man, but out of the corner of his eye he saw her pale face and big, frightened brown eyes. He hesitated.

"Come on, gimpy, give it your best shot," sneered his opponent.

That does it. Grant swung his fist toward the man's stomach, but Pete Davis grabbed his arm, blocking the blow.

"There'll be no fightin' on my ranch. This is a friendly gathering, not a barroom brawl. You two load up your horses and get out of here. You just wore out your welcome."

The younger man turned to Dawn, grasping her arm.

Grant tried to step forward, but Pete held him back.

"Come with me," said the other man. "I'll take you out for a night on the town. Show you how a lady's supposed to be treated."

She jerked her arm free and stepped back, glaring at him as if he had just slithered out of the grass. "You don't know the first thing about how to treat a lady. I wouldn't go anywhere with you."

Pete Davis cut in. "Ma'am, my wife can drive you home if you want her to."

Dawn shook her head and met Grant's gaze. She looked mad enough to eat fire and spit smoke. "He can take me home." She looked back at Pete. Her face had gone from white to fiery red. Tears welled up in her eyes. "I'm sorry, Mr. Davis."

"It's all right, ma'am. It's not your fault."

She nodded and jumped down from the hay, running toward the pickup.

Pete waited until the other cowboy stomped off, then turned to Grant and shook his head. "Hotheaded fool."

"Too big for his britches," Grant agreed.

Pete put his hand on Grant's shoulder. "I meant you. Go on home and cool off." He tightened his grip. "Don't let the past ruin your future," he said softly.

"I don't intend to." Grant's tone was sharp, and he hated the glint of hurt he saw in his friend's eyes, but he felt betrayed. Pete Davis and Wade were the only people he had ever confided in, the only ones who knew how deeply he had been hurt. Pete had known Susan and ought to understand why he had reacted the way he did. *Can't he see it's happening all over again?*

Grant picked up the cooler. He knew he had embarrassed Dawn, but anger and hurt kept him from caring. When he reached the pickup, she sat in the cab with her arms crossed, staring straight ahead.

Seething, he unsaddled the horses and loaded them and his gear into the trailer. When he climbed into the truck, Dawn didn't spare him a glance. Neither of them spoke until they were almost to Buckley. He felt her glare before she opened her mouth.

"What was that all about?"

He glanced at her and practically crushed the steering wheel in an effort to keep his voice low and controlled. "I was married to a flirt, and it turned out she did more than tease. I won't make that mistake again."

"I am not a flirt!"

"Oh, no? Then why were half the men there today trying to sit next to you?"

"They weren't."

"Yes, they were. They spent more time watching you than they did the competition—even the married ones. Lady, a man doesn't get that interested in a woman unless she's sending out signals."

She stared at him. "Signals! And just how did I do that?"

"Don't play so innocent. I saw you laughing at their stupid jokes and leaning close when they were talking to you."

"Only because I couldn't hear for the noise. They were explaining things to me."

"I just bet they were."

"Grant Adams, you've got a dirty mind."

He pulled to a stop in front of her house. "Maybe I do, but that's life in the real world. I learned it the hard way."

"Then I'm glad I don't live in that world." She pushed open the door and jumped out.

"You do. You just won't admit it."

Trembling, she flinched. "No, I don't. There's no need for your jealousy. There's no place in my life for a man who settles things with his fists." She slammed the door, tears rolling down her cheeks.

Grant didn't try to stop her as she ran to the house. That would have meant he cared, and he didn't. Wouldn't. In the end—and there was always an end—caring only brought pain.

Eleven

❧

Dawn tried to work out her anger and hurt by cleaning house. Vacuuming through tears wasn't too bad, but dusting and crying didn't mix. Exhausted, she fell into bed and tossed and turned until midnight, then she stormed around the house throwing things. Ranting and raving, she still had the presence of mind to make certain they were all unbreakable. Finally, she curled up in her big yellow chair with half a gallon of chocolate chip fudge ice cream and continued her talk with the Lord.

"I didn't do anything wrong! Did I? I don't know, Lord. The man is so messed up. I'm not sure anybody can help him. He's a hopeless cause." She ate in silence for a few minutes. "I know. Nobody's hopeless, at least not for you to help. But Lord, what am I supposed to do? He embarrassed the life out of me today. And scared me. He was actually going to fight that idiot because he thought I was flirting with him. The jerk only wanted to use me to meet Andi." She shuddered. "Lord, you know I can't handle violence."

Dawn looked down at the ice cream. If she took one more bite, she'd choke. "This is really stupid. I'll probably gain five pounds and go into sugar shock to boot." She put the ice cream away and went to bed, weariness overcoming her frayed emotions.

"Lord, if I was wrong today, please show me. I know I shouldn't have gotten angry and that a soft answer turns away wrath. I blew it on that one. Please help Grant to see that I'm not like his wife and that fighting is not the way to resolve conflicts. I really do like him, and I don't want our relationship to end like this. I want to trust him, not be afraid of his anger. Please heal his hurt and give him the faith to trust in you and in me. Help me to be patient and forgiving, and please give me the wisdom to understand how to at least be his friend."

When she climbed out of bed the next morning she felt as bedraggled as she looked. She dressed for church and waited by the front window, watching for Grant and hoping for a miracle. He never showed up, and she stayed home.

Shortly after noon, Wade and Andi dropped by. Dawn was tempted to hide and pretend she wasn't home, but she didn't. When she threw open the front door, Wade stopped and stared. Then he got mad.

"What did he do?"

"Good grief! Do I look that bad?"

"You don't look good," said Andi, stepping through the doorway. "What happened?"

"Did he try to take advantage of you?" Wade thundered into the room, acting like the big brother she never had.

"No, he didn't. Calm down, Igor. We had an argument."

Andi pointed Dawn toward the sofa and sat down beside her. "Start from the beginning."

Scowling, Wade sat across from them in the yellow chair. "And don't leave anything out. If I'm going to bust his nose, I want to know all the reasons why."

Dawn glared at him. "Is hitting the only way men know to resolve anything?"

Wade winced. "No, but sometimes it's a gut reaction. I wouldn't really hit him unless he tried to hurt you."

Andi frowned at her husband. "Do you actually think he might?"

"No, but stranger things have happened."

"You don't need to worry about that," said Dawn with conviction. "He might beat the guy I smiled at to a pulp, but he'd never abuse me."

Wade groaned. "Did he get in a fight?"

"Almost. It seems I was a bit too popular at the cutting yesterday—not hard to figure since I was the only single female there. Grant was gone for a while, competing and acting as herd holder. When he got back, this creep sitting next to me wouldn't move. He thought he was real hot stuff and provoked Grant. Grant was already furious and swung at the guy, but Pete Davis stopped him. Then he threw us off his property. I've never been so embarrassed in my whole life. Scared me, too. On the way home, Grant accused me of acting like his wife."

Wade shook his head. "I should have seen this coming."

"But I'm not like her, am I? I couldn't be rude to the people around me and ignore them. I laughed and talked with them, and I guess I flirted a little. It's just kinda natural." Tears sprang to her eyes. "But I don't think I did anything wrong. I wasn't trying to lead anybody on or anything."

"I'm sure you didn't," said Wade. "He's just paranoid. You're not anything like Susan. She was outgoing, too, but she was a temptress. Like Grant, I thought she was playing a part, that she'd never actually be unfaithful to him. Do you want to come out to the ranch with us? See if we can get him to come over and talk things out?"

Dawn shook her head. "I can't. I have to be at Mrs. Eden's birthday party in about an hour. I'm working in the kitchen, which is probably good. That way, not too many folks will see me.

"To be honest, right now I'm not sure I want to see Grant again. I don't know if I can deal with a man who gets into fights over something so stupid. If you want to call him and try to talk some sense into him, go ahead. Even if we don't see each other anymore, I don't want him to turn away from the Lord because of this. Don't let him lose his faith, Wade. He can do without me, but he can't do without God."

"I'll do my best."

Wade called her later that afternoon. "I talked to Grant a little bit ago, for all of a minute."

"Still snarling, huh?"

"That describes his mood. I think we'd better let the Lord work on him for a day or two. If you don't hear from him by Tuesday, let me know and I'll go see him."

"All right." Dawn sighed. "I'm going to skip choir practice and church tonight. I'm worn out."

"Have a good rest."

Dawn hung up and carried the cordless phone into the bathroom to keep it handy while she soaked in a hot bubble bath.

Afterward, she ate a bite of supper and read awhile. Grant didn't call. She told herself it was just as well—the man was nothing but trouble—yet her heart ached to hear his voice. She went to bed early, and as she drifted off to sleep, two phrases kept running through her mind: *Put your trust in the Lord. All things in his time.*

Business was slow in Memory Lane on Monday, but Dawn didn't mind. It gave her plenty of time to set up a couple of displays featuring Grant's things and rearrange others to hold more. She had taken almost a van load of items down to the store on Friday but had only had time to unpack one box and put the collectibles out. She wasn't surprised to see that several of them had sold on Saturday.

The day went by quickly because she was occupied. Though she could normally lose herself in the artistry of arranging displays, this time she kept one ear tuned to hear the phone. She had several calls, but none was the one she most wanted to receive.

At closing time, she went out the front, intending to walk home. After locking the door, she turned and found Grant parked in front of the next building. Joy leaped in her heart just at the sight of him.

With his arms crossed, he leaned against the fender of the truck, watching her carefully as she approached. "We need to talk," he said quietly, his expression solemn.

"Yes, we do, but I'd rather not do it on Main Street."

"Me, neither. How about if we pick up burgers and go back to your place?"

"That's fine."

Grant opened the truck door and assisted her as she climbed in, his fingers lingering on her arm after she was seated. When she met his gaze, Dawn saw her own longing and regret mirrored in his eyes. He lifted his hand as if to touch her face, hesitated, then dropped it to his side. Stepping back, he slammed the door and walked around to the driver's side.

The incident on Saturday was too big to pretend it hadn't happened. Neither of them tried to make small talk on the way to the drive-in restaurant. When they arrived at the Lazy Day, he asked what she wanted. She told him, and he placed the order through the intercom outside the window. The silence stretched out until it became unbearable.

"Did Kim get off to camp okay?"

Grant nodded, relieved she had initiated the conversation. "She called me right before she left. She was real excited."

"I only went to camp once when I was a kid."

"I never wanted to go, but I'm glad she gets to. I think Mom is ready for a week's vacation, too."

"She'll probably miss her like crazy by Wednesday."

"Maybe, but she and her gentleman friend have quite a few things planned. They've been dating for about six months. I think things may be serious."

"If they get married, how will it affect Kim?"

"Mom says she can keep right on living with them. John really likes her, so maybe it won't be a problem."

The carhop brought their food, and Grant paid for it, setting the bags on the seat between them and handing the drinks to Dawn. Again they rode in silence.

Back at the house, they chatted as they ate, but the conversation was strained. When they finished eating, Dawn threw away the hamburger wrappers and met his gaze.

"Living room?" he asked.

"Sure." She led the way, sitting on one end of the couch. He took the other. She kicked off her shoes and curled her legs up on the cushion, turning toward him. He shifted around at an angle so he could face her.

She waited.

He hesitated.

They both spoke at once, broke off, and laughed nervously. He held up his hand, asking her to let him talk first. "Dawn, there's no way I can apologize enough for what happened on Saturday. There is no excuse for the way I acted. I'm angry and disgusted with myself when I think how I humiliated and embarrassed you. When I think of how I must have frightened you, I feel sick."

"It did scare me. Grant, I can't be involved with a man who uses violence to resolve conflicts." Sorrow filled her golden brown eyes. "I just can't do it."

He tried to think over the thundering of his heart. *Please, God, let her forgive me. Let her believe I won't do it anymore. I won't, Lord. I won't!* "I understand, sweetheart. I should have realized what I was doing to you, but I was so jealous and mad, I couldn't think straight. I can't promise you I won't ever be involved in another fight, but if I do, it will be for a good reason, like protecting you. I give you my word that it won't be over something stupid like on Saturday. Can you forgive me?"

"Yes." She shrugged. "I do appreciate you rescuing me from creeps like what's-his-name. Just don't get carried away."

"I won't. You know I would never hit you, don't you?"

"I know you wouldn't. I knew that even on Saturday." She bit her lip and broke away from his gaze. "I'm sorry if I behaved improperly."

"You didn't."

She looked up at him, sadness in her eyes. "I flirted a little."

"Dawn, you did nothing wrong. There was nothing suggestive or improper in your actions. All you did was be your friendly, sweet self." He looked away. "I magnified everything you said or did and probably most of the things the men said or did, too. You're a pretty, vivacious woman. You were a new face and the only single woman there. It's only natural that those guys would want to talk to you. I was jealous and afraid." He finally looked back at her.

"What are you afraid of?" she asked gently.

"Of losing you before we get a chance to know each other." He shifted, laying his arm along the top of the sofa, and stared out the window. "I'm afraid that if I fall in love with you, I'll still lose you or fail you somehow and drive you away." He looked back at her and shrugged, embarrassed because he was being so open. *Now, she'll think I'm a wimp.*

"I have those same fears. I haven't been hurt the way you have, so I can only imagine how awful it would be. Still, I worry that I'll fall hopelessly in love with you and you won't love me, or that something might happen to destroy our relationship. But Grant, we have the Lord to help us. He can guide us and teach us."

He smiled wryly. "I've been bendin' his ear a lot since Saturday, and I guess he's been guiding me, too. With his help, I think I can change. I'm beginning to see and understand things better than I did before."

"That's good." She smiled. "It's also probably good that you didn't see the hissy fit I threw last night."

"I don't believe it."

Her smile became a grin. "Well, you'd better. I throw things when I get mad."

"Uh-oh. Are you going to charge me for anything?"

"Nope. Why do you think I have so many throw pillows?"

He groaned, then crooked a finger. "Come here."

She scooted across the sofa on her knees. "But I should warn you. If we keep having arguments, I'll gain a hundred pounds and charge all my new clothes to you."

He slid his hand around her waist. "Doesn't feel like you've gained anything to me."

"Guess I worried it off."

Cupping her jaw in his other hand, he stroked her cheek with his thumb. "Dawn, I'll probably get jealous again. I don't think I've licked it yet. I might get cranky and mad and say things I don't mean." He leaned toward her.

"I'll keep that in mind." She lifted her face to his, surprising him with a sweet kiss. Looking up at him, she slid her arms around his neck. "Grant, you don't have to be jealous of any man. I'm crazy about you."

"I hope so." As he drew her into his embrace, kissing her with all the tenderness he possessed, sunshine flooded his heart and beauty filled his soul.

Twelve

❧

On Tuesday afternoon, Dawn went out to Grant's ranch and spent several hours taking a cursory look inside more of the boxes. It seemed as if each one she opened contained something even more incredible than the one before it. Since these contained few things to discard, she decided to take them home to sort through. She was busy loading cartons in the van when Grant walked up.

Strolling into the bunkhouse behind her, he released a long whistle when he saw the dwindling stack of boxes. "You're really cookin' today."

She laughed. "I'm faking it. I scanned the contents and decided I could log them in and sort at home. Less time spent wrapping and unwrapping that way. I think we can sell most of what I have in the van." She motioned toward the furniture. "Now Alex's crew can pick up the jukebox and arcade machines, and we can haul the furniture and appliances to town. How should we handle that?"

"I'll rope Wade into helping me. We could make several trips with the pickup, but it might be smarter to rent a truck and haul it all at once." He studied the wood burning kitchen stove. "We may need extra help to move that."

"I'll leave the moving part up to you. Everything is in good shape, so it can all be taken directly to the store. Emily and I can have it cleaned up and polished within a few days."

He draped his arm across her shoulders. "You have a spot at the house ready for that Hoosier cabinet?"

"There's a spot, but Grant, you really don't have to give it to me."

He looked down at her and raised an eyebrow. "Are we going to rehash this again? I want you to have it, and that's final."

"Yes, sir."

"That's better. Now, say yes again."

She looked up at him. "To what?"

"Spending the rest of the day with me. We've both already put in a day's work. I think we should go play for a while."

"What do you have in mind?"

He swung around and put his hands at her waist, lifting her off the floor, laughing as she squealed and grabbed his shoulders. He carried her halfway across the room and set her on the sideboard that matched the dining room table. "Does it matter?" He slipped his arms loosely around her.

"It might. You have an interesting gleam in your eye, cowboy." She kept her hands on his shoulders.

"Nothing dangerous."

"That's good."

"I'd like to give you a tour of the ranch, even thought about going for a horseback ride."

Dawn's heart lurched. Just the thought of being so far off the ground sent icy shards of fear knifing through her. "Grant, I can't."

"I think you can." When she started to shake her head and protest more, he gently touched her lips with his finger. "Someday. We'll have lots of time to work on that. If you don't ever learn to ride, that's okay, too. Today, we'll just drive around. I left the pickup down by the barn. Ready to go?"

"You have to help me fill up the van first."

"No problem, since you've almost got it loaded." His gaze flickered to her mouth, then he straightened and lifted her down.

Dawn hoped her disappointment hadn't been written on her face.

After they loaded ten more boxes, Grant shut the van door and turned to watch her walk down the steps. Happiness enveloped her as a slow smile settled on his face. "What are you grinnin' at?"

"I was just admirin' the way the sunlight spins golden threads in your hair."

She almost tripped on the bottom step. "I think there's a poet hidden somewhere beneath that gruff exterior, Grant Adams."

He shrugged, but a tiny hint of color rose in his cheeks. "And it's liable to stay hidden, except maybe around you," he said, with a bemused expression. "You seem to bring out my romantic nature—the one I never knew I had."

She stopped beside him and linked her arm through his. "I like the sound of that. Let's see…I love chocolate of any kind, especially with nuts. Mums tend to make me sneeze, but I do pretty well with most other flowers. I especially like wild flowers."

They started walking toward the barn. "So now you expect me to do the candy and flowers bit?" he asked with a scowl.

"I'm just trying to make it easy for you by telling you what I like—in case you're ever in the mood to do something like that." She hugged his arm, resting her head on his shoulder for a second. "The nice things you say mean more to me than anything you could ever give me. It wouldn't bother me if you never brought me flowers."

A tiny smile lifted one corner of his mouth. "But it would bother you if I didn't buy you a box of chocolates now and then?"

"Well, I feel kinda silly buying them for myself."

"But you've done it."

She glanced up, liking the amused, happy sparkle in his eyes. "On occasion. I'm not one to let Valentine's Day specials pass me by."

"I'd bet there haven't been many Valentine Days you didn't have at least one love-struck swain bringing you presents."

"More than you think." She laughed at his disbelieving look. "About half the time I seemed to be between suitors on that particular holiday. The word's probably out that I like the giant-sized box of candy."

He surprised her by stopping suddenly beside the barn and pulling her hard against him. "If you're still putting up with me next February, I'll buy you the biggest box of chocolates I can find. But you'll have to share."

"I'm good at that." The words were hardly more than a whisper as she watched his eyes turn even darker blue.

"Yes, you are. You're good at a lot of things," he murmured,

148

slowly lowering his head. "Especially at bringing warmth and light to a cold, dark heart."

"Oh, Grant…" Her words faded on the wind as his lips touched hers in a lingering kiss filled with yearning. When he raised his head, she slowly opened her eyes. "It's a good thing we're not riding a horse. My legs are too weak to think about trying to climb up on one."

A glimmer lit his eyes, and he reached out one hand and unfastened the wide barn door. "You'll still have to do a little climbing." He shoved the door aside.

A soft nicker drew her gaze inside the barn. Smokey, a pretty gray horse with a black mane and tail trotted proudly over to meet them, pulling an old-fashioned buggy. He stopped and nuzzled at Grant's shirt pocket until Grant took out a sugar cube and gave it to him. "Have you met Smokey, my all around, do-anything-you-ask horse?"

"No, although Kim told me his name the other day." She gingerly patted the horse's neck, jumping a little when he turned his head toward her, but she kept running her hand down his silky coat.

"He's just lookin' to see if you've got anything good to eat."

"Sorry, fella, you'll have to talk to the man." When Dawn motioned toward Grant with her head, Smokey looked back at him expectantly. She laughed as Grant dug another sugar cube out of his pocket. "He understands English."

"Of course. They all do. Who else—besides the Lord—do you think I talk to all day? They even know a few Spanish words."

Dawn slowly walked around the buggy, tracing her finger along the shiny black wood and the black leather hood over the seat. The running gear was painted dark green to match the green leather seat. "It's beautiful."

"They've all taken real good care of it, including Mr. Ainsworth."

"It shows." She spied a blanket and an ice chest in the buggy boot and grinned.

"Didn't have a fancy picnic basket." He walked around to stand beside her. "Didn't think you'd mind."

"What I think is that you're the sweetest, most romantic man I've ever known." She stood on tip-toe and kissed him. "This beats the socks off a box of candy."

"That's in there, too. A little one."

"You're spoiling me."

"I'm working on it," he said, his expression serious. "I'm also trying to make up for being such an idiot last Saturday."

"Try no more, kind sir. 'Tis forgotten." She spotted the buckboard and chuck wagon over on the far side of the barn.

Grant smiled and stepped aside with a sweep of his hand. "After you, ma'am."

Dawn quickly inspected the wagons, practically jumping up and down in delight. "Grant, they're wonderful! Especially the chuck wagon—well used but still in good shape. They'll be perfect for the museum."

"How will you get them inside?"

"The loading dock has two huge doors, so moving them to the freight area won't be a problem. A contractor is putting in some big doors between there and the display floor to make moving things in and out of the main part of the museum easier. He and his crew are donating their time, so it will only cost us materials."

He smiled as they walked back to the buggy. "Now, I wonder who persuaded them to do that?"

"I merely asked." Laughing, she placed her hand in his, and he helped her into the buggy.

He chuckled. "I figured that's all it took."

"Have you talked to Pete Davis?"

"Went to see him last night after I left your place. He's a good man and a good friend. We're squared away." He walked around to the other side of the buggy. As he started to climb in, Smokey took a couple of steps forward, forcing Grant to hop on one foot. "Whoa! Stand still you mangy critter."

Smokey swung his head around and looked at Grant as if daring him to complain again.

He chuckled as he climbed into the buggy and picked up the reins. "We're not experts yet. I haven't driven this thing since I was a kid, and Smokey has only been at it since last week. You're doin' good, old boy. Real good," he crooned to the horse. 'That restored the animal's good humor, and he moved eagerly when Grant flicked the reins.

He guided him across to the road, and Smokey picked up the pace to a trot. "The first time I hitched him up, he balked like crazy, but now I think he actually enjoys it." Grant heard what sounded like a contented sigh coming from his companion. Glancing at her, his heart soared at her blissful countenance. "So how do you like it?"

"It's wonderful."

She looked up, her smile telling him she thought he was pretty wonderful, too. He decided the couple of times he'd almost gotten killed trying to teach Smokey to pull the thing was well worth it.

"We lost something when we started using cars. This brings us closer to nature, I think." Dawn took a deep breath and scanned the scenery. "I like the feeling of the wind and the soothing sounds of the horse's hooves and the wheels. You can see everything so well. I think I like that best."

"Downright pleasant now. I can see why beaus liked to take their sweethearts for a drive on a sunny day."

Pretending to wave a fan, she gave him a coquettish smile. "Bet it wasn't so nice on a wet day."

"Or a cold one."

"Except they could cuddle up to keep warm."

He smiled lazily. "Be my guest."

She glanced down at the six inches separating them and laughed. "I'm already pretty close."

"Not close enough."

She scooted over next to him. "Better?"

"Better. Want to drive?"

"Yes, but you'll have to tell me what to do."

He handed her the reins, keeping his hands on them, too. "Just keep a steady tension. We could probably let them drop to the floor, and Smokey wouldn't change pace. He's good about following the road even when it bends."

Grant gently released the reins and slid his arm around her. "Relax, sugar, he's too laid back to go too fast unless he gets spooked."

She glanced at him, her eyes wide. "Then what do I do?"

"Hang onto the reins until I have 'em, then hang onto the side of the buggy." He winked and she looked back at the road, relaxing somewhat.

152

"Sounds like you have a bit of experience in that area."

"We had a few skirmishes last week. A roadrunner dashed out in front of us and scared the wits out of my poor ol' hoss. He took off across the pasture with me bouncing around like a rag doll. Thankfully, he didn't go far."

"How far are we going?"

"Up on the mesa. The road winds up the other side. There's a little creek that runs along the base of it so Smokey can have a drink. Just follow the road until I tell you to turn."

"And tell me how to turn."

"Will do. Are you getting tired?" When she shook her head and smiled, he relaxed, stretching out his ornery leg. Hopping around on it before he climbed in the buggy made it ache mildly. It was a minor annoyance, one he paid little attention to.

His gaze returned to the mesa. His great-grandfather had courted his great-grandmother there. His grandfather had done the same with his sweetheart. So had his father. *Now me.* It seemed right to take Dawn there, especially in the buggy. They could see all of the ranch as well as the land he still hoped to regain. She understood that need. He wondered how many women would.

He'd never taken Susan up on the mesa. He'd never asked her because he knew instinctively she would have scorned the idea. They'd had times of true happiness but seldom at the ranch. He knew he should have been more sensitive to her feelings, instead of trying to bend her to his way of thinking. *Maybe if I'd bought her that house in Dallas she wanted, she'd have been happier and things would have been better between us.* He considered the possibility for a minute. *Likely not.*

"That was a mighty heavy sigh," Dawn said softly, looking at him.

He hadn't realized he'd made a sound. "Doin' some heavy thinkin'."

"Do you still miss her?" Dawn looked back at the road.

Tension radiated from her as she waited for his answer. He considered her question carefully. She deserved his honesty, but the answer surprised him. "No."

She shot him a glance, her brow wrinkled in a frown, but she waited for him to elaborate.

"I don't think I've actually missed her for a while now. When I think of her, it's to wonder what I could have done different, or if it would have mattered."

They were coming to the turn in the road. "You'll want to go left up there. Pull back on the reins a little to slow him down. That's it. Now, just ease the tension on the right rein and pull a tiny bit harder on the left." She negotiated the turn as if she had been driving a horse and buggy all her life. "Good. Couldn't have done better myself."

Dawn looked at the road that wound up the side of the mesa. "Your turn."

Grant gently took the reins from her hands, and she relaxed against the back of the seat. Slowing Smokey to a walk, he turned off the road. "We'll let Smokey have a drink before we head up."

He drew the buggy to a halt, then got out. "Want to stretch your legs a minute?"

"Sure." Dawn hopped out of the buggy, falling into step beside him as he led the horse down the shallow bank of the creek.

"You're not playing along, you know."

"How's that?" she asked, watching Smokey lower his head to the water for a long drink.

"In the olden days, a lady would have waited for her man to come around the buggy and lift her down."

Her man. I sure do like the sound of that. "I'll have to work on it. I'm bad about opening my own car door, too. Comes from dating guys who had forgotten how to be gentlemen."

"And here I thought you were just independent."

"Well, I'm certainly capable of jumping down from a buggy, but it's nice to have a man care enough to help me. I'll definitely need your help to get back in the thing."

Smokey finished drinking, and Grant carefully backed him and the buggy up until they could turn around. He spread his hands around Dawn's waist and lifted her up so she could easily reach the floorboard of the buggy. When she sat down, he grinned. "You know, our forefathers weren't so dumb. I bet they made buggies high on purpose, just so they could help the ladies."

"What if the lady was bigger than the man?"

"Then he'd have a problem." Grant laughed as he walked around to his side. "He'd probably have to invest in a portable step."

They zigzagged up the side of the mesa, reaching the top in a gradual climb. The view was spectacular. "It's beautiful!" exclaimed Dawn. "You can see forever."

"Just about. I'd be tempted to build a house up here, except it gets a double whammy when the wind blows."

Dawn shivered. "I can just imagine how it would be during a hard winter storm, plus it would be hard to go up or down. But it's lovely on a day like today. Thank you for bringing me here. The buggy ride is a treat in itself, but coming up here makes it extra special."

He lifted her down from the buggy and slipped his arm around her. "It's something of a tradition for the men in my family to bring the women they're courtin' up here. Started with my great-grandpa."

"Are you courting me, Grant?"

"Yes, ma'am. I do believe I am." His expression was serious, even guarded.

"I'm glad," she said softly, then stepped in front of him with her back to him. When he put his arms around her, she leaned her head against his chest and covered his hands with hers. "Is all this your land?"

"No. Most of it on these three sides belongs to me, but the ranch ends over there at that first fence. The Ainsworth place is on the other side."

"Is that some of what you want to buy back?"

"No." He pointed to the south. "See the far fence?" When she nodded, he continued, "There's another thousand acres on the other side that should be ours. Mr. Ainsworth has been good to let me buy back parcels whenever I can, even in little chunks. I won't borrow money to buy it. Bein' in debt is what lost it in the first place. If I can't pay cash, I wait."

"Someday you'll have it all." *I'll help you every way I can,* she thought fervently.

"I hope so, but that's a job to take on in the future. Right now, I'd like to feed my face."

Dawn laughed. "I thought I heard your stomach growling."

"It's been a while since dinner. Is this spot all right with you?"

"Perfect."

He caught her hand and spun her around toward the buggy. "That's the same thing my great-grandma said. I'll drop anchor while you set out the food."

Spreading out the blanket, she watched as he took a heavy cast-iron weight from the boot of the buggy. He carried it around in front of Smokey and dropped it on the ground. The horse anchor had a rope attached, which he tied to Smokey's bridle. It kept the horse from running away but allowed him to munch on the grass around him.

Within minutes they were hungrily devouring thick tuna sandwiches, chips, and chunks of cantaloupe. "You make a good sandwich, Mr. Adams."

He nodded and swallowed. "Thank you, Miss Carson. Would have been better with some of your homemade bread."

"Oh, I forgot! I brought you a loaf. It's in the van."

"In the front seat, I hope. Otherwise, it'll be smashed."

"It's safe." She polished off the last bite of her sandwich and grinned. "Didn't I hear you say something about candy?"

"Patience, my dear. Patience." He opened the cooler. "Here you are."

Taking the small box of rich chocolate candies, she carefully opened the top and held it out to him. "You go first."

"Do you have a favorite?"

She shook her head. "Love 'em all."

He took a mint and leaned back against a large rock, gazing at the scenery.

Picking a hazelnut chocolate from the box, she closed the lid and set it down next to the cooler, then moved over beside him. When he put his arm around her, she laid her head on his shoulder.

"A man could get used to this," he said softly.

"So could a woman." They were quiet for several minutes, enjoying simply being together. "Can I be nosy and ask you something?"

"Sure." His voice sounded lazy and contented.

"You may not like it."

"I'm still feeling penitent over Saturday, so ask away."

"Did you and Susan picnic up here much?"

"Never."

She turned around to face him, curling her legs up beside her. "You never brought her here?"

He shook his head. "Never even asked her. She wasn't happy at the ranch, and she wouldn't have been the least bit interested in coming up here."

"What a shame."

He shrugged. "I wasn't around all that much anyway, and when I was, I was busy with ranch work." He met her gaze, his eyes smoky blue and troubled. "I wasn't a good husband, Dawn."

"I expect you were better than you think."

"I hope so, but I could have done a lot better."

"At least you recognize your mistakes. Some people never do."

"I'm trying." His expression turned pensive. "There's another practice cutting on Saturday. Are you game?"

"I'm sorry, I can't go. I'm doing an antique show at the Six Flags Mall in Arlington. I'm leaving early Thursday morning so I can take some of your things to Alex to put in his shop. The show runs from Friday through Sunday afternoon, so I won't be home until late Sunday night."

"Were you going to bother to tell me you were leaving?"

She smoothed her fingers across his forehead and along his jaw, trying to erase his irritation. "Yes. With all that's been going on, I'd forgotten about it until I looked at the calendar this morning. I almost had a heart attack. It's a good thing I made my motel reservations a couple of months ago. This is the first time I've gone to this particular show, so it isn't ingrained in my mental schedule yet. I'd go with you if this wasn't already planned and paid for."

"I guess it's important to your business, but I'll miss you." He put his arms around her and drew her near.

"I'll miss you, too. I'll call every night."

"I can't hold a call in my arms, and kissin' a telephone receiver doesn't do a thing for me. Smoochin' with you on the other hand…"

The first kiss was sweet and gentle, but those that followed became increasingly more passionate, pushing them toward the brink of temptation. As he loosened his tight embrace, she forced herself to ease back. "Grant, we have to stop."

He nodded ruefully. "Before we fall off a cliff." He caressed her cheek and buried his fingers in her hair, gazing intently into her eyes. "Dawn, I didn't bring you up here to try and seduce you."

"I know you didn't," she said gently, smoothing his hair where she had messed it up. "You're a good man, Grant Adams."

A soft glow warmed his eyes, mingling with a trace of surprise. "You really think so?"

She leaned forward and gave him a tiny, quick kiss. "I know so. Now, come on. Let's get off this mountain before Smokey has to find his way in the dark."

"Smart as well as beautiful. My kind of gal."

Thirteen

❧

By Saturday night, Grant was climbing the walls. He'd spent the day at the practice competition, but enjoying the easy companionship of Pete Davis and winning the event had merely given him a respite from the loneliness eating away at his soul.

He thought he was accustomed to his isolated existence and had sometimes appreciated the solitude. But no more. The house had been far too quiet since Kim went back to his mother's. With Dawn out of town, loneliness seemed to hang in the air like a suffocating dust cloud.

He stomped out to the porch, letting the screen door slam shut behind him. "Don't have to be polite. There's nobody around to bother," he muttered. "Nobody to care." Sinking down on the edge of the porch, he stretched out his legs, absently rubbing his sore knee. He gazed up at the stars, picturing Dawn's sparkling eyes instead. "I never knew what lonely was 'til I met you. Not being able to hop in the truck and go see you is driving me out of my mind."

It didn't help that it was almost eleven o'clock, and she still hadn't called. He'd phoned her motel half an hour earlier, but she hadn't answered. Since then, his mind had tormented him with endless reasons why she wasn't in her room—or if she was, why she wasn't answering the phone. "Don't be stupid," he told himself in disgust. "You know her better than that."

Raking his fingers through his hair, he whispered the prayer he had already repeated a dozen times. "Please keep her safe, Lord. Don't let anyone or anything harm her. Send help if she needs it." He was too restless to sit, but his knee hurt too much to pace. So he hit the porch post with the side of his hand, not hard enough to do any harm to himself, merely to release some of his tension. "She'd better not plan on goin' off like this again." He knew he couldn't really demand that she not go to other shows, but he didn't have to like it.

The telephone rang and he jumped up, racing into the house. As he dived for the phone, his knee gave way, and he wound up on the floor with the receiver in his hand. Clenching his teeth against the pain, he couldn't say a word.

"Grant? Is that you? What's wrong?"

"Hi, sugar." His voice came out strained. Sweat trickled down his face and back. The stars had followed him inside and were frolicking before his eyes.

"Grant, are you all right?"

I am now. Her sweet voice wrapped him in comfort, and though it couldn't help the physical pain, it did wonders for the ache in his heart. "I will be in a few minutes. Stupid knee gave out. How are you? I've been worried."

"I'm sorry. I had a flat tire on the way back to the motel."

He forgot about his knee as visions of her walking alone in the darkness along the freeway ran through his mind. Then he pictured her on a side street, surrounded by gun-toting gang members. He didn't know if they had gang problems in that part of the Metroplex, but he figured any big city area was dangerous. "You didn't get out of the van, did you?"

"No, I stayed put with the doors locked and called my travel club on the cell phone. They sent someone out from a nearby gas station, and he changed it. I knew it was a flat because I'd hit a piece of scrap lumber a few minutes before. Guess it had nails in it. It fell off this old pickup that was ahead of me, and I couldn't avoid it because of oncoming traffic. I don't think the guy even knew he lost it. Anyway, everything is fine now."

"I'm glad you didn't try to change it yourself." He was also a little surprised, since she had an independent streak a mile wide.

"I would have if I'd been out in the toolies or in familiar territory, or maybe even there if it'd been daylight. Under the circumstances, I didn't feel safe out of the van. A carload of rough-looking characters had passed me earlier. They drove by again after I had the flat. I watched them in the mirror and it looked as if they were about to turn around until they met a police car. He pulled up behind me and they kept going."

Thank you, Lord! "I kept askin' God to keep you safe."

"Thanks. Believe me, I was praying fast and furious about then, too. The policeman stayed until the service station man showed up, so I know the Lord was watching over me." She paused. "I miss you."

He leaned back. It was simpler and much less painful at the moment to lie down on the floor instead of trying to get up. "I miss you, too. You're still comin' home tomorrow night, aren't you?"

"Yes. I should probably get home about eleven or so."

"Be sure and call me when you get in. Otherwise, I'll stay awake all night."

"I hadn't figured you for the worrying kind."

"I didn't used to be." He never had worried about Susan, and now he wondered why. *I was too young, too self-centered to think about it. And too trusting.* "Now I know there's a big, bad world out there. How is the show going?"

"Sales are good, and the promoters say tomorrow afternoon should be our biggest day. Otherwise, I'd head home early. How was the cutting? Did you win?"

"Yep. We waltzed through. And my friends are still speakin' to me, so I guess I didn't do too much damage last week."

"I'm glad. Did Kim have fun at camp?"

"Had a great time. She called this afternoon right after she got home. She sounded tired but still excited. Since you won't be here tomorrow, I'm going to San Angelo to see her and Mom and go to church with them." He laughed softly. "My normally calm, sedate mother let loose with the best Rebel yell I've heard in a long time when I asked about going to church with her. She knew I'd accepted the Lord, but I honestly don't think she ever expected me to set foot in a church. She was quick to assure me that I didn't have to dress up."

"I'm glad you're going with them. Alex and Rita are taking me out to breakfast, then we'll catch the early service at their church. I'll be finished in time to reach the mall and set up before the rush starts."

"Good. Maybe we can go to church together next week."

"I'd like that. How's your knee?"

"Aches, but it's not throbbing anymore. I'll take a pain killer when I head off to bed. Guess I should have taken more time to answer the phone." He gingerly stretched his leg.

"It only rang twice. Where were you?"

"On the porch."

"Grant! No wonder you hurt yourself."

"Just anxious to hear your voice, sweetheart."

"Well, I would have let it ring."

"I know. I've been thinkin' about something, and I'd like your opinion."

"Sure, what's up?"

He pictured her curling her legs up beneath her and that special way her eyes widened in anticipation. "I'm thinkin' about having Kim move out here. I know she wants to, and I think we could probably manage now that she's older. I'm afraid she'll be lonesome without her friends, and it'll mean a twenty-mile bus ride to school."

"Do any of your neighbors have kids near her age?"

"A couple of families have some boys, but they're about five miles away. There's nobody close enough for her to visit on her own, even if she wanted to."

"Are you willing to play chauffeur?"

"I'm willin' to try, but I doubt if I'd be able to take her some place every time she wants to go."

"Most parents can't go every time their kids want to do something, and they probably shouldn't anyway. Kim's pretty mature for her age. Why don't you discuss it with her? Maybe even do it on a trial basis with the understanding that if she's unhappy she can go back to your mother's? She'll make new friends at church, too. We have quite a group of kids around her age." She paused.

"And when I'm around, she could always hang out with me for a while if your schedule and hers didn't mesh."

"You mean that? I don't intend to saddle you with her, but it's nice to know she'd have some place to stay if I got stuck and couldn't pick her up at a certain time. I don't expect it would happen often."

"Yes, I mean it. I like your daughter."

Enough to be her mama? He bolted up to a sitting position, thankful he hadn't spoken out loud. Yet he had told Dawn he was courting her. He swallowed hard. Even if Kim didn't come to live with him now, he would want her to if he married again. He'd want them to be a real family. But would Dawn? "If she's living here, it'll make it harder for you and me to be alone."

She giggled. "Ever heard of hiring a baby-sitter? I believe teenagers still watch over kids so adults can go on dates. Besides, it'd probably be a good idea if we had a chaperon around some-times," she said, her voice suddenly sounding all soft and dreamy.

He knew she was remembering their picnic. He doubted he'd sleep a wink, now that he was thinking about it, too. "Spoil all the fun."

"Not necessarily, but it might keep us out of trouble."

"Yeah, it might."

"I'd better go. We both have an early day tomorrow."

"Don't forget to call when you get home."

"Yes, General. Sleep tight and don't let the bed bugs bite."

"Hey, I'm a better housekeeper than that." He told her good night and hung up the phone. Hoisting himself up to his chair, he glanced around the living room. Papers and magazines were piled everywhere. A pair of dirty socks, each rolled up into a tight ball, were still in the corner where he had thrown them at a spider on the wall the night before. A dirty shirt, one he thought he had worn on Thursday, lay on the back of the couch. A glass, empty TV dinner container, and two empty pop cans—one crushed, one not—sat on the table beside his chair.

He looked in the kitchen and winced. A week's worth of dirty dishes were piled in the sink, and two pairs of boots sat by the back door, wearing various levels of barnyard debris and dirt. "At least I took 'em off and didn't track it all over the house." Checking the kitchen floor, he decided it wouldn't have mattered much if he hadn't taken them off. "When did I get to be such a slob?" The answer was simple, he realized, as he hobbled into the kitchen.

When I started living alone.

He dragged himself out of bed near sunup the next morning. After breakfast, he spent a couple of hours cleaning house. It wasn't spotless when he headed for the shower, but it did look considerably better. At least Kim wouldn't scream and run the other way if she came home with him.

His knee was swollen and sore when he woke up, but it was throbbing by the time he quit cleaning. After his shower, he sat in the recliner for ten minutes with an ice pack draped over his knee. Then he wrapped it with an ace bandage and put on his newest pair of jeans and the light blue, striped Western shirt his mother had given him for his thirty-third birthday a few months earlier.

Right before leaving the house, he downed more ibuprofen and picked up his Bible from the dining room table. His gaze fell on a cane propped up next to the old sideboard. He knew he'd be smart to take it but hated using it and drawing attention to himself and his infirmity. Walking across the room he decided that he wouldn't fall on his face, even though his leg hurt.

When he arrived at his mother's house, Kim raced out to meet him. She wore a pretty red dress and white sandals, and her long hair hung freely down her back instead of bound in the usual braid. He suddenly realized that in all too short a time she'd be a young woman instead of a girl. He made up his mind then and there that she was going to live with him. He'd missed far too much of her childhood already. When she got old enough to start dating—say around eighteen or nineteen—he would be the one to meet her beaus at the door with a firm handshake and stern expression.

He carefully climbed out of the truck, leaned down, and gave her a bear hug, lifting her off the ground. "Whoo-ee, gal, when did you get to be such a pretty young lady?"

She giggled and hugged his neck. "Instead of a cute-as-a-speckled-pup tomboy?"

He laughed and hugged her harder. "It'll have to be a pretty tomboy from now on, 'cause you done left cute in the dust." He set her on the ground and took her hand when she held it out to him. "Gotta go slow, dumplin'. I kinda banged up my knee last night. Oh, wait a minute. Almost forgot my Bible." He reached inside the truck cab and picked up the book from the seat, then shut the door.

As they walked toward the house, his mother came to the door, opening the screen. "Did you hurt that knee again?"

"Yes, ma'am." He released Kim's hand and she ran on inside. Smiling at his mother, he bent down to kiss her cheek. "Guess that's what I get for actin' like a teenager and divin' for the phone."

Meg Adams raised an eyebrow. "This Dawn woman must be special."

"She is." He smiled gently at her amazed expression. "You'd like her, Mama."

"Well, Kim certainly does, but I'll make up my own mind when I meet her. Which had better be soon."

"Yes, ma'am. How about next Sunday afternoon? Maybe we could drive down after church."

"I'd like that, son." Her eyelids fluttered and she turned away.

Grant saw the tears glisten in her eyes. "What is it, Mama?" he asked, resting his hand lightly on her shoulder.

She waved her hand in the air and shook her head. "Don't mind me. I'm happy that you've found a nice woman to date, and I just can't get used to you talking about going to church. It blesses me so to know you've found the Lord." She turned back around and laid her hand against the side of his face, patting it gently. "And the last time you called me Mama was when you woke up in the hospital after that bull tried to make hamburger out of you."

Grant laughed and pulled her into his arms. "I love you, Mama. Thank you for stickin' by me through everything."

"You're my son, Grant. I'd never turn you away, no matter what," she said, hugging him back. "Now, let go so I can fix my face. Can't go to church with a red nose and smeared mascara."

As she walked away, Grant thought of Wade and how his mother had chosen her career over her family. Their broken relationship still caused Wade deep pain. *Thank you, Lord, for my mother. Thank you for her goodness, unselfishness, and unfailing love.*

Since Grant's leg was hurting, his mother decided they should skip Sunday school and only go to the worship service. After the long drive from the ranch to San Angelo, he appreciated the time to elevate and rest his leg, knowing he would get more out of the service if he wasn't in great pain.

As they pulled into the parking lot, she glanced at him. "Are you all right, son?"

"It's the first time I've been in church since I was a kid. I'm as nervous as a settin' hen at a coyote convention."

She laughed and squeezed his shoulder. "There's nothing to be scared of."

"Dawn said that at her church they introduce the visitors to the congregation. Do they do that here?"

"No. You can just sit incognito in the pew."

"Good." He even managed to walk in without limping dramatically, which eliminated more of his uneasiness.

Meg's gentleman friend, John, was waiting in the foyer. Smiling like a proud papa, he shook Grant's hand. "Good to have you here, son."

"It's good to be here, sir." Grant hung onto Kim's hand as if she were the adult and he were the child afraid of getting lost in a crowd.

As they followed his mother and John into the sanctuary, Kim looked up at him and smiled. "It's fun, Daddy. We even have a guy who plays the guitar and another who's really hot on the drums."

He smiled, thinking church had changed since he was her age. He was surprised to discover just how much. The choir sang a lively song that set his foot to tapping, and a little later a young

170

woman sang a solo. While not done perfectly, it still touched his heart with its simple message of faith. When the white-haired, elderly preacher stood up, Grant braced for a fire-and-brimstone sermon, until a gentle smile softened the man's angular features.

From the moment the minister began to speak in his deep, dramatic voice, relating how the apostle Peter was miraculously freed from prison by an angel, Grant was enthralled. He grinned at the way the man told the story and could picture the angel nudging Peter awake and telling him to be quiet so he wouldn't wake the two guards to whom he was chained. Then he marveled at how the shackles fell free, the angel led Peter out of the prison past guard after guard without them seeing him, and the gate to the city swung open by itself.

Grant's mind wandered a bit at that point, as he considered how God was leading him out of his own personal prison of bitterness and guilt. He hadn't passed through the last gate yet, and sometimes he felt as if he were moving toward it by inches. Seemed like every time he made a bit of headway, something came along to shove him backwards. There were still obstacles to overcome on his journey, but the chains binding him to the past had been broken. For that alone he was profoundly thankful.

They didn't stay long at church after the service, although people were friendly and made him feel welcome. He was a little uncomfortable with all the fuss, and his mother seemed to sense it.

She had left dinner cooking in the oven, so shortly after they arrived home, they sat down to roast beef with potatoes, carrots, and gravy. Home grown green beans, icy cold watermelon cubes, and banana cream pie rounded out the meal. They all pitched in to clean up afterward, and in no time, John and Kim were busy playing badminton in the back yard while Grant and his mother sat in lawn chairs on the porch and watched.

Grant watched his mother laugh at her beau as he teased Kim. He knew he'd made the right decision about Kim coming to live with him. It was time his mother had a life of her own, without kids to raise. Still, it would be hard on her to let her granddaughter go, and he didn't quite know how to bring up the subject.

Meg glanced at him, then gave him her full attention. "Looks like you're doin' some mighty deep thinking over there."

He grinned. "Too deep for such a shallow mind." His gaze went back to Kim as she giggled and did a little dance after tying up the score. "I've really missed having Kim around this week. That old house just echoes with emptiness." He looked back at his mother with a tiny frown. "I'm tired of being a part-time daddy. I want her to come live with me."

Meg's eyes misted as she nodded. "It's time. She wants to live with you in the worst way. She needs you, and you need her."

"Yes, ma'am, I do. But I know it's not going to be easy on you."

"I'll miss having her here, that's for sure, but I'm gettin' too old to try to keep up with that child."

Grant shook his head. "You can run rings around me, and you know it. But I think you've got other things you'd rather be doing at this point in your life," he said, with a gentle smile and a glance at John. "When are you two going to get married?"

"Soon." Meg's brow creased in a frown. "But that doesn't mean Kim can't live with us. You're not doing this because you think we don't want her here, are you?"

"No. I'm doing it because I love her. I want us to be a real, everyday, live-together family. I don't want to miss any more of watching her grow up." He hesitated, then admitted, "I'm tired of being alone."

"She can't ease all of your loneliness. Only a loving wife can do that."

"I know." Grant looked out across the yard, watching Kim play but not really focusing on her. Instead, he saw Dawn's lovely face teasing him with her smile, beckoning him with the loving warmth in her eyes. Turning back to his mother, he said quietly, "Guess I'm workin' on that, too."

"Glory be! You're actually thinking about marrying again?"

"Just considering the possibility, that's all. Don't go shoutin' hallelujah or shopping for a new dress to wear to the wedding. I've got a long way to go before I'm ready to take that step, if I ever do. The thought scares the living daylights out of me."

"I understand. I've enjoyed John's company, but it's taken me quite a while to reach the point where I can honestly say that I want to marry him. I loved your father very much, but he was not an easy man to live with."

"I know."

"After being on my own all these years, I didn't want to lose the freedom to make all my own choices, good or bad. I wasn't sure I could handle the responsibilities, sacrifice, and possible heartache that might come with marriage. I'm still not sure how well I'll do, but he's a good man. I love him, and he loves me. That's worth a powerful lot."

"Yes, it is." *But is it enough?*

Fourteen

❧

W oman, be careful with that paint brush," growled Grant.

Dawn looked over her shoulder as he leaned away from the brush she was absently holding up at shoulder level. "Don't sneak up on me, or the rest of your face might accidentally turn yellow," she said with a laugh. She pointed toward the opposite wall. "I thought you were using the roller over there."

"Finished, and I've got enough paint on me already, thank you very much."

She turned toward him, waving the brush beneath his nose. "I don't know about that. Those are awfully small specks. I think you need a big dab of yellow right there." She pretended to try to paint his nose then dodged as he grabbed for the brush and missed.

"I don't know how I let you and that kid of mine talk me into paintin' her room. I have other things I should be doing."

Giggling, Dawn backed up as Grant stalked her across the room. "Oh, sure, like taking Dancer for a ride. That's not work."

"It is, too. He needs the exercise." He smiled as she discovered she had backed into a corner. "Just because I enjoy it doesn't mean it's not work. Now, give me that brush."

She tucked her hand and the brush behind her. "Nope. I'm keepin' it for self-defense."

"Self-defense, my foot. You're planning on using it for offense. I can see your mind workin'."

"So now I have little wheels and cranks sticking out of my head?"

"No, but you've got a gleam in your eye." He stopped in front of her—within inches—and reached around her back, clamping his hand over her wrist.

"So do you."

"My brain's working, too, but I'm not thinkin' about paint," he murmured.

Here she was in her grubbiest clothes, yet every time she had glanced his way all morning, he had been watching her as if he couldn't get his fill of looking at her. She willingly relinquished the brush, barely noticing when he tossed it onto the nearby roller tray. Slipping her hands up his chest and around his neck, she asked, "So what's on your mind, handsome?"

"Same thing that's usually on my mind. You."

"And is that good or bad?" She almost purred when he put his arms around her and drew her against him.

"A little of both. I'm glad you're home, but it's been way too long since I kissed you." He lowered his head slightly.

"Over a week." She stretched up on tiptoe.

"Roughly eight days and nineteen hours."

"And sixteen minutes. Roughly," she whispered, her lips a heartbeat away from his.

"An eternity," he breathed, closing the tiny distance between them with a heated kiss.

Dawn lost all sense of time and place, rejoicing at being where she belonged—in his arms. She loved him. Any lingering uncertainty had vanished on her arrival when she saw his tender, welcoming smile. He deepened the kiss, and her legs turned to mush. Clinging to him, she returned his ardor with all the love in her heart.

"All right, Dad! Way to go!"

Grant jerked his head up. He took a step back but, to Dawn's relief, kept his arm around her. If he hadn't, she was afraid she might have crumpled into a little ball at his feet. A blush rushed up her neck to her face, and his cheeks flushed a dull red beneath his dark tan. As one, they looked toward the doorway where Kim stood grinning at them.

"Hey, don't mind me. I'll go watch TV or something." She turned and disappeared down the hall with a giggle and an exuberant, "Yes!"

"Now we've done it." Grant looked up as if asking for divine help.

Leaning her forehead against his chest, Dawn tried to think of something profound to put his mind at ease. Instead she erupted in a fit of giggles.

"I'm not so sure this is funny."

She looked up, meeting Grant's scowl with another burst of laughter. It took a minute to stop and catch her breath. "I'm sorry, but that was a scene right out of a TV sitcom," she said with a grin.

His fierce expression faded and a twinkle sprang up in his

eyes. "All we needed were hoots and wolf whistles from the audience."

"I think I heard a few."

He leaned down, resting his forehead against hers. "Have I told you lately how beautiful you are?"

"Grant, I have on the grungiest clothes I own, and I'm covered with paint."

"And you're still beautiful. You were wearin' a lot more paint the first time I saw you, and it didn't keep me from thinking about you." He straightened. "I almost didn't go to that benefit dance because I was so irritated with myself for wanting to see what you looked like all dressed up. I hung around on the edge of the crowd, hoping to catch a glimpse of you."

"I was running around all over the place, so that should have been easy."

"Not until you went up on stage to welcome everyone and start the show." Threading his fingers in her hair, he caressed her jaw with his thumb. "You were so beautiful and full of life. You took my breath away. I stood in the shadows and watched you dance with one guy after another, and I envied them all."

"Why did you wait so long to ask me to dance?"

He dropped his hand. "I didn't know if you'd even remember me, and I didn't want you to think I was some guy from the crowd trying to make a move on you. When I saw you standing by Wade, I figured that was a good time to show up, especially when you were being bumped around."

"I was very glad to see you, and not just because you made a good barrier between me and the rest of the crowd. I'd been looking for you all night. I felt awful because I had to go work in the concession stand and couldn't dance with you." She slid her arm around his waist. "You didn't really think I wouldn't remember you, did you?"

He shrugged. "I don't figure I'm too memorable."

"Oh, honey, how can you think that?" She laughed and squeezed him so hard he exhaled with a *whoosh*. "You practically gave me heart palpitations that day at Wade's. I was thinking about you so much that I didn't even remember driving home."

He looked down at her with a self-satisfied grin as he put his arm around her. "Really?"

"Really. Come on, we'd better go wash out the brush and roller before the paint dries."

"And show my daughter that we ain't misbehavin'." He released her and walked over to the paint tray, handing it and the roller to her. He picked up the brush and moved across the room to pick up the can of paint.

"She knows we won't get too carried away."

"How's that?" He shoved the lid down tight on the can.

"That first Monday when I came out here to work and she was here, we had a little discussion about you and me."

Straightening with the paint can in his hand, his gaze narrowed. "What did you talk about?"

"I let it slip that we'd had a date. It surprised her."

"It should have. I don't date. Didn't date."

"Anyway, I explained that you'd hurt your knee, so we stayed at my place and had pizza and talked. She asked if you spent the night and if we'd slept together."

"She what?" he roared, almost dropping the can.

"Shhh. I admit I was shocked, but kids today see all kinds of things on television or have friends who have those situations going on at their house. She was polite about it and very relieved to learn we hadn't. Actually, that led to a discussion about the Lord. It was all very interesting."

"I'll bet it was." He shook his head. "I expected her to ask you some questions but not quite anything so personal." A frown crept across his brow. "Or so grown up. She's just a kid. She's not supposed to know about that kind of stuff."

"They grow up fast in today's world."

"Now I know she's not datin' until she's twenty."

Dawn laughed and reached up and ruffled his hair. "Sure."

They found Kim watching television and eating a peanut butter and jelly sandwich. She didn't say a word, just smiled when they came into the room.

"I'll go wash out the paint stuff," he said.

Dawn glanced at Kim, but she was watching cartoons. Looking at Grant, she silently mouthed, "Chicken," and made a face. He gave her a smug smile and escaped out the back door. Hoping to ignore the whole thing, Dawn went into the kitchen to make sandwiches for lunch.

Kim joined her thirty seconds later. "See, I told you Daddy likes you. Guess you like him a lot, too."

"Yes, I do, but sweetie, don't read too much into a kiss." Dawn smiled. "Even a humdinger like that one. There needs to be a lot more to a relationship than physical attraction."

"Oh, sure, I know that." Kim pulled a bag of potato chips from the cabinet and sat down at the kitchen table. "Like what?"

"Friendship, respect, love, and trust. Believing in the same things—at least the important things—helps, too."

"You guys got all that, don't you?"

"We're making a good start, but it takes time to get to know and understand a person."

"How much time?"

"I don't know." *Not long, I hope.*

"Grandma said Daddy got hurt real bad when him and Mom split up."

"Yes, I think he did. He loved your mother very much. When a person loses someone they love, it's hard to take that risk again."

"You mean 'cause he's afraid of gettin' hurt?"

"Yes."

"If somebody's heart gets hurt, how do you fix it?"

"With plenty of patience and understanding and a lot of love." Dawn glanced up at Kim, who was staring thoughtfully across the room. "Something troubling you?"

"It must take somebody special to fix a heart that's been hurt so bad, 'cause me and Grandma love Daddy more than anything, but he still looks sad sometimes." She smiled at Dawn. "But not as much since you two started datin'."

"Well, that's good to hear." Dawn cut the sandwiches in half and prayed for wisdom. "But I expect a big reason your daddy isn't so sad is because he's found Jesus. I bet he'll be even happier now that you're living with him."

"Grandma says he won't be completely happy until he gets a new wife who loves him more than anything."

"That's something only your daddy knows."

"So you probably shouldn't try to be his new wife unless you love him more than anything. Do you?"

Dawn sputtered, trying desperately to think of a suitable

answer. The back screen door squeaked, and Grant came swiftly into the room. His expression indicated that he had heard much—if not all—of their conversation, and he wasn't happy about it.

"Kim, you're out of line. Apologize to Dawn." Grant glanced at Dawn's stricken face and felt his temper rising. She looked more upset than when he'd opened the door. With effort he banked his anger and fixed his gaze on his daughter. She looked like she might cry any minute. *Great! Now, I've got two unhappy females on my hands.* "Kim," he said more gently. "I think you have something to say."

She hung her head, then looked at Dawn. "I'm sorry."

Dawn reached across the table and squeezed the girl's hand. "Apology accepted. I know you were only looking out for your daddy."

Kim nodded, obviously trying very hard not to cry. Grant pulled out a chair and sat down at the table. "Come here, honey." She got up and slowly walked over next to him, looking as if she expected him to yell at her or something.

"I love you," he said, hugging her, holding her long enough for her to know he meant it. When he relaxed his arms, she pulled back and looked somberly at him. "Sometimes in life, you have to be patient and wait to see what happens," Grant said. "Marriage is serious business, and it takes time for two people to figure out if they're right for each other. I know wondering what's going on is hard on you, but you have to wait and not ask so many questions. Give us time to come up with the answers. Okay?"

She nodded. "Sorry, Daddy."

He hugged her again. "It's all right, baby. This is one of those growin' up lessons. Why don't you run down and see Mitzie, but don't be gone too long. I expect we can start moving your things back into your room soon."

"Okay." Kim smiled and bounced out the back door, but the tension in the room remained.

Grant glanced at Dawn. She appeared to be as uncomfortable as he was. "Are one of those sandwiches for me?"

She nodded and handed him a sandwich on a plate. Then she put the bag of potato chips between them on the table.

"Thanks. Want a pop?" He strolled over to refrigerator, trying to pretend nothing had happened.

"Sure. Got grape?"

"Yep. Keep plenty on hand." *Since I know you like them.* He wondered why he found it hard to admit that out loud. He handed her a grape soda and took a cola for himself then sat back down.

They ate in silence.

Total, agonizing silence.

Grant took a bite of apple-filled cookie, then dropped the rest on his plate. Shoving back his chair, he stood and walked quickly around the table, taking Dawn's hand and pulling her to her feet. He wrapped his arms around her in a tender embrace without attempting to kiss her. He only wanted to hold her, and for her to hold him. "You know I care for you, don't you?"

She threw her arms around his waist as if she never wanted to let go and nodded, her curls brushing his jaw.

"And you must care for me a little, because you keep hangin' around."

She laughed softly. "You know I do, you big dolt."

He tightened his hold as his heart shouted at him to say the words he longed to, but couldn't. A big knot blocked his vocal cords and set his heart to hammering. He had climbed on the meanest bulls with grim determination, but he couldn't tell a pint-sized dynamo that he loved her. The realization made him tremble with yearning and fear. Fear won.

When he heard Kim skipping up the porch steps, humming to herself, he quickly released Dawn and stepped back. Not looking at her, he grabbed the potato chip bag and rolled down the top, fastening it with a clothes pin. Dawn silently picked up their plates and set them in the sink.

Kim came through the door. "Okay to come in now?"

"You bet. Ready to move your bed and dresser back into your bedroom?" Grant tugged on her long braid.

"I'm ready." She raced ahead of him down the hall.

Grant met Dawn's gaze, relief flowing through him when she smiled. She reached out and took his hand as they followed Kim down the hall, and he called himself a fool for being such a coward.

They worked hard for the next couple of hours, first hauling out the dropcloths from painting, then setting up Kim's room. She had asked Dawn to help her redecorate, and Grant was amazed at the transformation of the place. He'd never given much thought to it before, since Kim had only stayed with him on occasional weekends and some in the summer. She had never complained, and he figured the bed and old three-drawer chest had been sufficient. Until he took the old curtains down, he hadn't noticed they were the same ones he'd used in that room when he was a boy. He'd been ashamed when they literally fell apart in his hands.

He had bought a new twin frame and mattress, but she wanted to keep the old iron headboard. She had also rejected his offer to buy her a new dresser, choosing instead to use a dresser and chest of drawers that had belonged to Aunt Lena. They had brought all her things from his mother's the day before, including her desk and a bookcase.

After they moved the furniture into the room, he set up her small stereo, stretching the speakers to each side of the room as she requested, while Dawn and Kim unpacked books and other treasures. Finished with the stereo, he hung a shade above the window and put up a shiny new brass curtain rod.

"Honey, can you help me move the mattress?" Dawn asked, as he stepped down from the small step stool.

Surprised and pleased because she used the endearment in front of his daughter, he smiled. "Rearranging the furniture already?"

"No," she said with a laugh. "We forgot to put the dust ruffle on the bed before we put the mattress on it. It covers up the springs."

"I knew that," he said, his grin telling her he really hadn't known any such thing. All he needed were sheets, a pillow, and a couple of blankets. He didn't even own a bedspread. He lifted the mattress off the bed and leaned it against the wall. "Want me to hang the curtains?"

"Thanks." Dawn flashed him a smile while Kim looked up in surprise. He laughed, tweaking his daughter's nose. "Don't worry, I can tell the bottom from the top." He picked up a white eyelet curtain from where it lay draped over a chair and held it out in front of him. "Does it make any difference which side I put this on?"

"No, it's the same on both sides."

While Grant hung the curtains, Dawn and Kim put the dust ruffle on the bed. He lifted the mattress back into place. "Now what?"

"We'll make the bed and put down the rugs. I think we're about done."

"I'll take these boxes outside and put away the stool." He stuck the stool in the pantry and carried the cardboard boxes out to the trash barrel, which was about thirty yards from the house. Mashing them flat, he shoved them into the barrel, added the previous day's newspaper, and lit it on fire. Dropping a wire mesh screen over the top, he waited a few minutes to make sure everything was burning, then went into the house.

When Grant stepped into Kim's room, he couldn't believe his eyes. A beautiful wedding ring quilt of varying shades of blues mixed with yellow topped Kim's bed above the white eyelet dust ruffle. White eyelet pillow shams covered the bed pillows, and one bright yellow and three dark blue throw pillows were tossed artistically across the head of the bed, along with an assortment of stuffed animals. The ones she had gotten from the bunkhouse seemed to have a special place of honor against the headboard.

A wide blue rug ran alongside the bed, a plush spot for a little girl to set her toes while she wiggled into her slippers on a cold winter morning. Her desk was neatly organized, as were the shelves of books beside it. The tiny cowboy and cowgirl figurines perched proudly on top of the bookcase.

Several old, cobalt blue bottles in varying shapes sat on a white doily on one side of the old-fashioned dresser next to a beautiful old hand mirror with a bouquet of roses painted on the back. Kim's straw cowboy hat hung from one corner of the dresser mirror, an oddly comforting focal point in a room that was an amazing and wonderful mixture of old and new, little girl and tomboy, and budding femininity.

"Do you like it, Daddy?"

"It's beautiful, princess. It suits you perfectly." His gaze met Dawn's, and he didn't even try to hide his amazement. "Thank you."

"You're welcome." She stepped up beside him. "It does look good."

He put his arm around her and pressed her against his side. "I can't believe the difference. Is that one of Grandma's quilts?"

Dawn nodded. "We ran across it a couple of days ago, and Kim fell in love with it."

"Dawn gave me the blue bottles and hand mirror, Daddy. Aren't they neat?"

"Yes, they are. The perfect touch." He looked at Dawn, thinking that she seemed to have the perfect touch with just about everything. "I think we'll go sit down for a while."

"I'll see how my stereo works."

"Not too loud."

"Sure, Dad."

Grant guided Dawn down the hall to the living room, offering her the recliner.

"You go ahead. I'll curl up here." She kicked off her shoes and plopped on the couch, leaning against one arm and stretching her legs out in front of her. "Feels good to sit down."

He took the recliner, silently thanking her since his knee had started protesting again. He raised the footrest and sighed in relief. Then he looked around and dismay washed over him.

He'd cleaned up the house, but now he felt as if he were really seeing it for the first time.

"Grant, what's wrong?" asked Dawn with a small frown.

He shoved his fingers through his hair and sighed again, this time in exasperation. "This house. I never paid any attention to it before, but with Kim's room lookin' so good, the rest of it ought to be condemned."

She laughed. "It isn't that bad, but it could use some sprucing up."

"A lot of sprucin' up." He felt overwhelmed. He didn't like painting, but he could handle it. Figuring out how to do the rest was a major challenge, one he wasn't sure he wanted to take on. *It'll be expensive to fix this place up right. Take a chunk out of my land money.* He pictured Kim bringing home her friends and felt embarrassed at the thought of them seeing the dirty walls, threadbare rug, and lumpy old couch—the one Dawn was sitting on. He almost groaned out loud. *What good is having all the land if the house isn't fit to live in?*

Suddenly he felt ashamed and sick at heart. This was where he'd brought Susan. It hadn't been in quite as bad a shape when she was here, but he'd never gotten around to doing any more than buy her new, modern furniture. True, she had never asked to have the house repaired; a fancy home in Dallas was more her style. She probably would never have been happy at the ranch, but he should have tried to improve the place instead of staying so focused on his goal that he was blind to what was needed.

He wasn't going to let Kim feel ashamed of her home. It wouldn't hurt if it took longer to buy back that last thousand acres. At one time the house had been an important part of the ranch, one that should never have been neglected. *Daddy couldn't help it,* he thought. *He was just trying to hang on, but I can take care of it.*

Dawn surprised him by silently walking over and perching on the chair arm next to him. "You're awfully quiet over here."

"I want to fix up the house, really do it up nice. I want Kim to be comfortable bringing her friends here, not ashamed because everything is so run-down." He scanned the room and frowned. It looked hopeless. "My granddaddy built this house. Maybe it's too old to try to redo. Do you think I should build a new one?" That would mean going into debt—something he had promised himself he would never do.

She studied the room. "How's the wiring?"

"I had it rewired when I bought the place. I was afraid not to. Dad replaced most of the plumbing over the years as one part after another went bad. I think structurally it's sound, and I had a new roof put on a couple of years ago."

"So mostly it's cosmetic, although you really should get new appliances. I haven't seen a pink range in ages. You might be able to sell it at the store as a collectible."

He laughed, reaching up to take her hand. She closed hers around it, resting them both on her thigh. "I was knee-high to a grasshopper when Mama bought that stove. She was so proud of it. I don't know, maybe I should keep it. The oven and two burners still work."

"Spoil yourself. Get a self-cleaning oven."

He let his jaw drop. "You mean ovens are supposed to be cleaned?"

"Once in a blue moon. You probably wouldn't know what to do with a frost-free refrigerator, either."

"Aw, come on. It's fun to chisel off the ice to shut the freezer door."

"You haven't been chiseling much. That icebox looks like an iceberg."

Again, he feigned surprise. "Ain't it supposed to?"

"No, hayseed, it ain't." Her gaze drifted around the room again, a soft light glowing in her eyes. "It could be a beautiful home. You have plenty of space. Aunt Lena's dining room table and sideboard could go right there," she said, pointing at an empty corner of the big living room.

"That's where Mama had her dining room table. We used to open it way out at Thanksgiving and Christmas and fill it up with food and people all around."

Her fingers tightened on his as her eyes widened with that excited anticipation he loved. "You could put the tall, narrow pie safe next to the kitchen. It would be like adding another cabinet."

She shifted slightly, looking toward the television sitting on its cheap stand. "And I have an old school cabinet at the shop that would be perfect as an entertainment center. At one time it had dozens of thin shelves to hold papers, but now it has one sturdy shelf in the middle and a smaller one on the bottom. You could put the television in the top section and your video recorder and stereo amplifier and cassette deck on the bottom. It has two glass doors, but we'd probably have to take the top one off."

Suddenly, she blushed and ducked her head. "Listen to me run on. I'm sorry. I shouldn't be telling you how to redecorate."

When she tried to pull her hand away, he held tight and wound up tugging her off the chair arm onto his lap. "I want to hear your ideas. I'll hire someone to do the painting, maybe those high school kids you said helped at the store. But I don't know how to begin to make this disaster into a nice home."

"It already is. A home is built with love, not pretty things. Now, if you want to make it look nicer, you bring in a decorator." Her eyes gleamed with excitement.

"You applyin' for the job?"

"I'm no expert."

"I like your place, and I like what you did with Kim's room. Besides, I don't think you'll charge me an arm and a leg," he said with a grin.

"You know I won't charge you anything."

He laughed and hugged her, then supported her back with his arm. "I was hoping you'd say that. Not that I'm a cheapskate, but I'd like to think you'd do it because you'd enjoy it." *And because you want this to be your home.*

"I will enjoy it, but you'll have to help. I'm not making all the decisions."

"Do I have to go shopping?"

"For some things." She patted his cheek. "Don't worry, honey, you can handle it. I'm not about to spend tons of your money without your approval."

"Tons?" he croaked. "I don't need a gold-plated recliner."

She pulled some stuffing from a long crack in the vinyl chair back. "No, but you need a new one. In fact, the only furniture in this living room you should keep is the pie safe and the desk."

"The rest is pretty pathetic. I found most of it at the second-hand store."

"It could run into money."

When she pushed herself upward, trying to get out of the

chair, he gave her a gentle boost. He watched as she prowled around the room, nibbling thoughtfully on her thumbnail. No doubt her mind whirled with ideas. Love welled up in his heart, flowing sweetly through his whole being. "We'll keep it within reason, but we're going to do it right."

With God's help, hopefully, I'll do everything right—even love you.

Fifteen

❦

Once Grant decided to refurbish his home, he charged full speed ahead. A bit amazed by his enthusiasm, Dawn happily jumped into the project with him. They decided which furniture in the bunkhouse he should use, then made lists of things to buy and what should be done. Two days after finishing Kim's room, the three of them set off to Sidell in Dawn's van, armed with a long list.

They stopped first at the appliance store. Having discussed their needs ahead of time, Grant spent less than an hour purchasing a new refrigerator, range, and, to Kim's surprise and delight, dishwasher. He teased Dawn by asking the salesman if he had anything in pink but settled on white. He arranged to have the appliances delivered in a few days, and they were off to the furniture store.

Choosing furniture for the living room took longer. Dawn watched his eyes light up when they walked through the door and he spotted a dark green leather sofa. Looking at the price tag, he winced and moved on, but his gaze kept going back to it. They walked all over the store, testing first one couch and then another. It seemed as if the ones that were comfortable all came in fabrics that weren't suitable or patterns that Grant didn't like.

Dawn took him by the hand and led him back to the green leather sofa. "Sit."

He sat down and sighed wistfully.

She sat beside him and bounced a little on the cushion. "Sweetheart, this one has your name written all over it."

"Can't afford it."

"The price isn't the only thing you should consider. It's not all that much more than some of these others. The leather will last a long time and be easier to keep clean than fabric would be. That's important when you've got kids and cowboys traipsing through."

He chuckled. "You sayin' we're a dirty bunch of scalawags?"

"You do tend to get dusty. Kim and her friends probably will, too, and you don't want to always be asking her to keep off the couch. It's the most comfortable sofa in the store. Your friends will appreciate that."

He frowned. "I don't have many friends. Hardly anybody ever comes out to the house."

"Do you invite them?" she asked gently.

"No." He appeared embarrassed. "Guess I never have been too sociable."

"You don't need to be a party animal, but it's nice to have a comfortable place for people to sit when they do visit, even if it's just Wade and Andi or your mother and John."

"It probably will last longer." He looked at Kim as she came up and dropped down on the sofa. "What do you think?"

"I like it, Daddy. It feels better than those other ones. You gonna get it?"

"I'm thinking about it."

"While you're thinking, you can pick out a new recliner," said Dawn. "That old one is going to the dump. It's a wonder it doesn't make your back hurt. Have you ever noticed the way it leans to one side?" They walked toward the chair section of the store.

"No, can't say that I have," he said, lowering one shoulder so that he leaned against her.

Kim giggled and Dawn laughed until he dropped a quick, little kiss on her temple. She looked up at him in surprise and was almost undone by his expression. It went beyond tenderness, but was it love? She couldn't make a sound. He smiled gently, as if he understood, and put his arm around her shoulders, keeping her by his side. For the next few minutes she couldn't form a coherent thought.

Grant took his time choosing a recliner. Kim got bored, so he sent her off to look for a coffee table and end tables. He settled on a dark brown recliner with leather where the body touched it and matching vinyl everywhere else. He had Dawn test the slightly smaller ladies' chairs. When she found one she liked, he promptly told the salesman he wanted that one, too. She started to protest, but he silenced her with a look.

"If I have a comfy place for you to sit, maybe you'll hang around more often," he said softly.

"More? I'm practically living there now," she said, with a grin, thinking how much time she'd spent at the ranch in the past weeks.

An odd little smile touched his face. "So I've noticed."

Dawn went weak all over, and she sank down on the chair, mumbling about testing the cushion again as the salesman asked

Grant a question. She hadn't regained her composure by the time Kim came back and grabbed her father's hand, leading him off to look at tables. He glanced at Dawn, but she waved him on, pretending to be interested in a lamp. *Father, don't let me see things that aren't there. Help me not to love unwisely or to push him.* Her mind knew she must be cautious, but her heart defied logic with a cry all it's own—*please, Father, let him love me.*

When she rejoined Grant and Kim at the other end of the store, she was pleased with their choice of tables. Made of heavy oak, the tops were inlaid with dark green and cream quarry tiles. "Those will be great. They're nice and sturdy. You can set glasses and hot cups of coffee on them without worrying about it ruining the wood. Did you find them, Kim?"

The girl beamed. "Yes. See, the end tables have another shelf and the coffee table has this neat part with doors so you can hide stuff."

Dawn laughed. "What are you going to hide there?"

"Probably all the junk on the top when company comes," said Kim, covering her mouth with her hand as she giggled.

"Sounds good to me."

Grant decided to buy the sofa, and armed with a matching swatch of leather, they headed off to buy carpet. After much discussion, they decided on a sculpted beige with flecks of varying shades of brown and green. They grabbed a burger for lunch, then shopped for ready-made drapes and new bathroom rugs at the large department store at the mall.

As they carried their purchases to the van, Kim looked up at Grant. "Are you going to buy a new bed and curtains and stuff for your room?"

"No, I'll wait a while."

"Daddy, your mattress sinks in the middle, and you don't even have a bedspread or a comforter and dust ruffle." Kim looked at Dawn and shook her head. "He just has a couple of scroungy old blankets, and you can see the springs and cobwebs under the bed. There's no curtains, just a window shade that's so old it's yellow."

"It's always been yellow."

"That's because it's been there for a hundred years."

"Not quite. Those blankets are warm in the winter and the air conditioner works, so I've got no complaints. I'll keep my door shut, so you won't have to look at it."

"Aw, Dad, you ought to fix your room up as good as mine."

"I'll do it later, punkin." He looked over Kim's head, capturing Dawn's gaze and holding it. "When the time is right."

Dawn's cheeks grew warm, but she read the hope in his eyes and tucked it away in her heart. If she helped him redecorate his bedroom, they would be doing it as a couple, either married or soon to be.

Tired, they drove back to Dawn's and ordered a pizza. After dinner, Kim curled up in the big overstuffed chair to watch an old movie, while Grant and Dawn went out to the back yard. Instead of sitting on the porch, Grant sprawled on the grass and Dawn sat down beside him.

"I talked to your friend Mark yesterday," said Grant. "He's lining up a couple of his high school buddies to help him paint. They plan to start on Monday."

"Did you get the paint?"

He nodded. "Antique white. I'm going to have them do the whole house, except for Kim's room, of course. George Jackson at the hardware store was telling me about putting new doors and fronts on the kitchen cabinets. Costs a lot less than replacing the whole thing."

"I've seen some that were done that way. They looked brand new. And your cabinets are fine, just a little worn."

"We can have it all done through the hardware store. New sink, cabinet top, the works."

"Sounds like the way to go. What about the bathroom? You aren't going to throw out that old clawfoot tub, are you?"

"No. I'll keep it. Works great for soakin' a sore knee, although I use the shower most of the time. That was another thing I had put in when I bought the house. Lost the linen closet, but it was worth it. Jackson's Hardware has bathroom fixtures and cabinets, too. The selection in the store isn't very big, but he has catalogs and can get things from a warehouse in Sidell overnight. I have to stay home and work tomorrow, but I thought I'd come into town Saturday and arrange to have the kitchen and bathroom done. Want to help me pick out cabinet styles?"

Dawn hesitated. Shopping together in Sidell had been no problem, since no one knew them. If she went to Jackson's with him and started picking out bathroom cabinets, half the people in town would know about it before nightfall. A good portion of them, regardless of her sterling reputation, would assume she was moving in with him. The others would be looking for the wedding announcement in the local paper and stopping her on the street when they didn't find it. "I think I'd better leave that up to you. Besides, I have to work Saturday. We've had a lot of customers come through lately."

He took hold of her hand. "Afraid of gossip? Don't want to have your name linked with mine?"

"Folks already know we're dating. I even brag about it." She smiled at him, hoping he would understand and not be hurt. "But you know how some people can be."

"The curse of small towns. Everybody thinks they know everybody else's business, and when they don't, they assume the worst or make up tales."

"I'm sorry, Grant. I don't want to disappoint you, but I don't want to feed the rumor mill. Those old coots, er, gentlemen who meet down at Greene's every morning have finally quit harping about my foolishness for opening the store. I don't need them— and all the other gossips in town—pointing out the error of my ways, even if my sins are only figments of their overactive imaginations."

"I could bash a few heads," he drawled. "Knock some sense into them."

She knew he didn't mean it. "It would never work. They're too hardheaded."

He sat up, cradling her face in his hand. "I understand, sweetheart. I know talk can hurt, and I don't want you hurt." He feathered a gentle kiss on her forehead. "Not ever."

On Sunday morning, Grant and Kim picked Dawn up in time to go to Sunday school. He was even more nervous than he'd been when he went to church with his mother. This was where he hoped to attend for many years to come. It was also the church in which Dawn had grown up. Many of the people here knew him, if not personally, then by name and reputation. No doubt they had heard as many bad things about him as good.

Sensing Kim's uneasiness as they walked toward the building, he placed a comforting hand on her shoulder. "Doin' all right, punkin?"

"I'm kinda scared 'cause I don't know anybody."

"I'm a little nervous, too, but we know Dawn and Wade and Andi."

Kim perked up. "And Wade's Aunt Della and Uncle Ray."

Dawn looked around Grant and smiled at Kim. "I have a friend I think you'll like. She's just your age. I told her you were coming." She nodded toward a girl with short, light brown hair standing outside the church door. "She's waiting for us. Her name is Mary Beth Taylor, and she lives between your ranch and Wade's. She loves horses, too."

Grant looked at her in surprise. "I didn't realize Shep had a daughter, although I have seen him with his boys. I didn't know he was a churchgoer, either."

"They haven't been coming long. Shep and his wife, Carolyn, are a couple of Andi's recruits. They heard her sing about Jesus that night at the benefit concert. Carolyn was so touched she came to church the following Sunday. The next week Shep and the rest of the family came with her, and they've been attending ever since."

"That song got to me, too." He looked down at her and smiled. "Reckon I was a little more hardheaded than Shep."

"Maybe you just needed someone to give you a nudge."

"Could be."

When Dawn introduced Kim and Mary Beth, the two girls hit it off at once. A minute later they headed toward their Sunday school class. Dawn hooked her arm through Grant's. "That was easy."

"I expect I'll be wearin' out the pavement between the Taylor place and mine. I'm glad she found a new friend so quickly. Thank you for making it happen."

She shrugged. "Kim is such an outgoing girl, she would have done fine on her own. I thought I might make a few points with her dad if I made things easier for her."

Grant laughed. "Well, you made the points all right, but you'll never convince me that's why you did it."

"Believe what you want," she said with a teasing smile.

Wade and Andi walked up, welcoming Grant. "Glad you made it." Wade introduced him to a couple of other men standing nearby. When they heard his name, he sensed they were surprised to see him, but they gave him a warm welcome.

He talked with Shep Taylor for a few minutes, who was excited to see him and to learn that Kim was living at the ranch.

"My Mary Beth gets mighty lonesome for a girl to play with. She can hold her own with the boys, but she'll really enjoy having a friend all her own."

"It'll be good for Kim, too. I've been worried about her missing her friends in San Angelo. She's done pretty well so far, but she hasn't been there but a week."

Shep winked at Dawn, then looked back at Grant. "I want to know how an ornery cuss like you latched onto such a sweet, pretty lady."

Grant laughed. "I'm still tryin' to figure that out." He met Dawn's gaze. "But I'm sure glad I did."

Wade leaned over close to them. "If you two can quit starin' at each other, we'll go on in to Sunday school."

Dawn elbowed her friend in the ribs. "Be nice, Wade

Jamison. I didn't harass you two when you were dating."

"Yeah, right." Wade laughed and dodged her elbow. He draped his arm around his wife's shoulders. "Should we refresh her memory, darlin'?"

"We'd be here all morning."

Grant watched as Andi looked at Dawn, and the two cousins burst into laughter. He met Wade's amused gaze. "Now we're in trouble."

"Yep. These two are worse than schoolgirls. We'll have to keep them separated or they'll be at it all during Sunday school."

They walked down the hall to one of the adult classes. When the four of them filed into a row of chairs, Wade made certain he and Grant sat between the two women. Dawn and Andi pretended to be highly insulted, with Dawn proclaiming that Andi should rap Wade's knuckles with her pen if he and Grant talked during class.

Grant figured Wade sat next to him because he wanted to help him feel comfortable. With Wade on one side, Dawn on the other, Shep Taylor in front of him, and a few other familiar faces in the group, most of his uneasiness disappeared. The class was studying the book of Proverbs, and he found it fascinating.

As they went toward the sanctuary after Sunday school, Grant came across several more people he knew. They all seemed genuinely glad he was there. During church, Andi sang a solo, and Grant was almost moved to tears by the beauty of her voice. Yet he knew the power of the song alone did not cause his great swell of emotion.

A still small voice spoke to his heart, telling him he was where God wanted him and that he was welcome there. He looked down at his lap, where his hand firmly held Dawn's, and silently thanked God for that reassurance. He thanked him for his grace and love and for the acceptance of the church members. Most of all, he thanked God for the woman sitting next to him, for her strength of character, her sweet and gentle spirit, and for her loving heart.

Make me worthy of her, Lord.

Sixteen

❧

The next few weeks flew by as workmen turned Grant's house upside down. Kim spent most of her days with Mary Beth or Dawn to escape the noise, dust, and fumes. Grant caught up on all sorts of projects around the ranch, dropping by the house several times during the day to make sure everything was going as planned. They ate out or with Dawn or with Wade and Andi. A couple of times they drove into San Angelo to see his mother.

The last time, Dawn went with them. She liked Meg Adams immediately and sensed that the older woman also liked her. When Grant ran Kim over to her friend Jenny's for a while, Dawn stayed with his mother. Meg showed her pictures of Grant as he was growing up. When they reached the section of high school snapshots, Dawn laughed. "Oh, my, I bet he drove the girls wild."

"Sometimes I wondered if those gals hadn't planted a homing beacon on him. We'd go to the grocery store and they'd show up, making a fuss. We'd go to the mall and here would come another bunch of them." Meg shook her head. "It worried me, the way they fawned over him. A boy can only resist temptation so long when it's being thrown at him. That was one reason I held my tongue when he got married so young. He was only twenty-one.

"Looking back, I realize I should have counseled him against it. She was only twenty and starry-eyed over the daring, handsome, wild-bull rider, but I don't know if she ever truly loved him."

There were several pictures of Grant at the rodeo—climbing onto a bull's back in the chute, riding in what even Dawn could tell was perfect form, accepting trophies and checks, and one where he was waving his hat to the crowd. In that particular close-up he was smiling, but his eyes held no joy. Puzzled, she looked up at Meg. "Had he just won?"

"Yes. One of the biggest purses on the circuit, by riding one of the meanest bulls. He came out of that event completely unscathed."

Under Meg's watchful gaze, Dawn studied the picture. "He should have been jubilant and excited, basking in the glory." She looked up with a frown as understanding bloomed. "But he wasn't after the glory. He didn't love the thrill, did he?"

"No. He did it for the money, plain and simple. He was a natural and was determined enough to be the best. When we lost the ranch, it ripped open that boy's soul. He'd always been a loner; that place was his whole life. It was all he ever dreamed about. He'd started in the rodeo even before he got out of high school and went into it full time right after graduation.

"My husband had died the year before, and though I had a good job, Grant sent me money every month. Then when Kim came to live with me, I quit work until she started school, and he supported us completely. He's turned a profit on the ranch from the very first year. Even after I went back to work, he still helped plenty and made sure we had everything we needed."

"He's a good man."

"Yes, he is, and he needs to hear it from somebody besides his mother."

Dawn smiled, not minding Meg's forthright manner because it showed she cared about her son. "I've mentioned it a time or two."

"Good. Anymore than that and he'll either get a big head or won't believe you. By the way, I earn more than enough to take care of myself and my fiancé is well fixed, so I told Grant not to send me any more money."

Dawn turned the page, coming upon a snapshot of Grant and his wife. Pain stabbed her heart, a jumble of jealousy, longing, and regret. She could not stifle her envy of the beautiful woman at his side, no more than she could quench her yearning for him to look at her the way he was looking at Susan. Yet overshadowing both feelings was deep sorrow that someone who had loved so much had been hurt so badly. "She was very beautiful."

"Yes, she was."

"He loved her very much." Dawn struggled to keep her voice even, but she knew she could not hide her turbulent emotions completely.

"Yes, he did, but he can love again. In fact, I think he's well on his way already."

Dawn jerked her head up. She had hoped, even thought, he was falling in love with her, but after seeing that picture, she wasn't sure. "I don't know."

"I do." Meg patted her arm. "I doubt if he can admit it yet; not sure if he realizes it. He's older, wiser, and much more cautious, but you mean a great deal to him. I see it whenever he looks at you or talks about you."

"I hope you're right."

As Grant pulled into the driveway, Meg plucked the photo album from Dawn's lap and tucked it away on the bottom shelf of the coffee table. "I'm always right, dear," she said with a knowing smile. "Just give him the time he needs."

A few days later, Grant helped Dawn move the rest of Aunt Lena's boxes to her house, where she finished sorting and pricing. Leaving what they would use in the ranch house, he and Wade loaded most of the other furniture in their pickups and brought it to Memory Lane. Alex was sending out a truck the next day to pick up the jukebox, arcade machines, and some other things. With Wade's help, Grant proudly delivered the Hoosier cabinet to Dawn's kitchen. Wade quickly bade them farewell and raced off to a committee meeting at church.

Grant stood back, surveying the cabinet and room with a grin. "It looks like it was made to go there."

"That spot was designed for one just like it," said Dawn, slipping her arm around his waist and fighting back tears. She leaned her head on his shoulder. "It's perfect, Grant. It's been empty there for way too long. I'm thankful I have Grandma's house, but it never seemed quite right without her cabinet. Somehow, that vacant space always reminded me that she's gone, too."

He wrapped her in his arms and held her, letting her deal with the memories in her own way. When she took a deep, shuddering sigh, he asked softly, "Better?"

"As long as I'm right here." She snuggled a little closer, wanting to stay in his arms forever.

"I kinda like it, too." There was a trace of huskiness in his voice. He kissed her forehead. "Want to go out to dinner? We never did make it to that Chinese place."

"What about Kim?"

"She's spending the night with Mary Beth." When she looked up at him, he smiled. "So you have me all to yourself."

She was in a strange mood, one that could land her in a heap of trouble if she wasn't careful. She lowered her gaze, afraid he would see her vulnerability and her need. In spite of his mother's assurance, the picture of Grant and Susan haunted her, leaving her uncertain and afraid. She desperately needed to know he loved her, to hear him say the words, to feel it in his touch. She wanted him all to herself, not just for the evening, but for the whole night. *Lord, don't let me make us stumble.*

Pulling away, she walked around the kitchen, picking up items at random. "I'm not very hungry. I couldn't do justice to a Chinese dinner." She moved to the Hoosier cabinet, setting the items inside without a thought to what went where. "In fact, I'm really tired, so maybe you should just go on home. I won't be very good company." She started gathering up another handful of things while he watched her through narrowed eyes.

With two swift strides, he blocked her path. "Dawn, what's going on?"

"Nothing. I'm just in a weird mood."

"Nothing. That's why you're decorating your new cabinet with that ugly orange plastic scrubber thing you use on the dishes." He plucked the scratcher from her hand and threw it into the sink. "There's nothing wrong, but one minute you're holding me like you never want to let go, and the next minute you're showing me the door." Anger edged his voice, but he didn't raise it. He took the collectibles from her hands and carefully set them on the table. "What happened to all that honesty? Did you suddenly decide it didn't count with me?"

She closed her eyes. "It counts."

"Right." Grant wanted to yell and pound on something to startle her into looking at him. But he didn't want to frighten her, not ever again. He took a deep breath and forced himself to calm down. "Dawn, look at me and tell me to leave," he said quietly. "I'll go, but I deserve to know the real reason."

She slowly lifted her gaze to his, as if the very action were painful. "Don't go," she whispered.

He drew in a harsh breath as he looked into her heart. Intense longing, desire, and perhaps love shimmered in her eyes, interwoven with uncertainty and the cold glint of fear. *Is she afraid of what might happen if I stay?* He watched the myriad emotions rush across her face and realized she was, but it wasn't all that troubled her.

Moving slowly, he put his arms around her, fighting the temptation to pick her up and go find a bedroom. *Father, help me to be strong. Give me wisdom.* "It'll be all right, sweetheart. I'm not going to leave, and I promise we won't do anything we shouldn't." He felt some of the tension drain from her body.

Now what? Swiftly, as if God sent a message directly from heaven, he understood what she needed most and what he had to do. Clearing his throat, he eased back. "I think we'd better sit down and have a talk."

She glanced up, then quickly looked away, nodding hesitantly, and led the way to the sofa. When she sat down on one end, he almost took the other, then decided against it. He sat in the middle, turning at an angle to face her. "Dawn, you know I care for you very much, don't you?"

She nodded without looking directly at him.

"You don't look real convinced," he said gently. "Have I done something to make you doubt it?"

She shook her head.

"Has something happened to make you doubt it?"

Her gaze shot to his, and she chewed on her lip.

He shook his head and sighed. "Honey, for a gal who can talk a mile a minute, you're being awfully quiet. This is not the time to clam up. Come on, tell me what's wrong. Honest and direct."

She took a deep breath, clenching her hands. "When we were at your mother's the other day, she showed me some pictures of when you were in school and in the rodeo."

Grant went still, wracking his brain, trying to remember what was in that photo album. He thought it still held some pictures of Susan because they had decided Kim should be able to look at them whenever she wanted.

Dawn glanced up, then looked back down, folding the hem of her hot pink, cotton shirt a few turns, then smoothing it out, only to fold it up again. "There was a picture of you and Susan. She was sitting on a picnic table, and you were standing beside her."

He knew instantly which picture she meant, and his heart sank. He had never loved his wife more than at that particular moment.

"She was so beautiful, and the way you looked at her…" Her voice cracked. "It would be impossible for you to love anyone else the way you did her."

Grant reached over and captured her hand, partly to stop her from ruining her shirt but mostly because he needed to touch her. "Dawn, that picture was only a tiny fragment of time. I had just found out a few minutes earlier that I was going to be a daddy."

"And somebody took a picture?" she asked with a frown.

"We were in her folk's backyard. She'd been with her mother when she got the call from the doctor. Her mom is a camera nut, so after I calmed down a little, she snapped that shot from the porch with her telephoto lens."

He put his arm along the back of the couch. "I loved Susan, and in spite of the anger and hurt on both sides, I wanted to make our marriage work. But that's all in the past.

"I wish I could get down on one knee and ask you to marry me, but I can't...and it's not just because my knee doesn't work right. I still have some hang-ups, some things the Lord is helping me work through, but we're not there yet. I can't make a commitment or ask you to make one until I know I can see it through for a lifetime. I have to be sure of myself."

"And of me," she said gravely, slipping her hand from his.

"Yes." He rubbed his hands over his face. "There's a part of me that's still afraid, that keeps reminding me that if one woman left me, you might, too."

"I wouldn't."

"I want to believe that, more than anything. But it's not you. It's me. I guess what it comes down to is that I failed Susan, and I'm afraid I'll fail you."

"You won't." Her voice was soft but firm with conviction.

"I pray every day that you're right." He cupped her chin with his hand. "I may still be messed up in some ways, but one thing I know for certain. I love you with all my heart."

She threw her arms around his neck and buried her face against his throat. "I love you, too." She raised her head, her gaze locking with his. Tears glistened like stars in her lashes. "I'll always be here for you. I believe in you and love you with every breath I take. I'll wait for you to get everything straightened out, but please don't take long. I have a real problem with patience, and I've already waited a lifetime for you to come along."

Laughing—and closer to crying than he would ever admit—he crushed her to him, kissing her with the joy of love proclaimed. Slowly their kisses grew longer until Grant reluctantly raised his head.

Resting her head against his shoulder, Dawn smiled up at him. "I expect now would be a very wise time to go putter around the kitchen."

He watched the laughter and love play across her face and wanted to shout with happiness. "You got a miniature golf course in there I don't know about?"

She laughed and shook her head. "I suppose we could put some glasses on the floor and try to hit grapes into them with the broom."

"Waste of good grapes. I'd rather eat 'em. Which reminds me, what are we going to do about dinner?"

"I have one package of macaroni and cheese left."

"That'll do. As long as we don't play Nintendo afterwards."

"Kim still stomping you?" Dawn stood and headed for the kitchen.

He followed. "Every night. You'd think I could beat a ten-year-old kid." He reached up in the cabinet for a couple of plates. "Guess my mind hasn't been on the game."

"More likely you just need to do something a little more your speed. Maybe like a game of gin rummy?" She filled a pan with water and set it on the stove.

He couldn't resist her teasing, challenging grin. "It's been awhile, but I used to do all right."

"A while, huh? Pete Davis told me you two have been gettin' together for a game of rummy once or twice a month for the last couple of years."

"We were. Been a little busy lately."

"He also said you beat him on a regular basis." She ripped open the macaroni and cheese box and took out the sauce mix.

"Well, if he gets to talkin' about horses, he's easily distracted." He set the silverware on the table.

She opened a drawer and pulled out a deck of cards. "You can talk about horses all night and it won't distract me." With a wide grin she shuffled the cards faster than a dealer in a Las Vegas casino. "Look sharp, cowboy. You've just met your match."

Laughing, Grant dumped the macaroni into the boiling water. "Yes, ma'am. I do believe I have."

Seventeen

❧

Before they knew it, the last two weeks of July rolled around, and Grant left for the Cutting Horse Derby. On Monday, the first afternoon of the event, Dawn waited anxiously by the phone at the store for him to call. He had taken Dancer and Gus to Fort Worth the day before so the horses would be well rested from the trip before the competition began. They had talked for an hour Sunday night after he settled in at the hotel, and he had called again early that morning to tell her he wouldn't be riding in the first go-round until the afternoon.

She had caught up on the bookkeeping that morning, but after noon she was too antsy to sit still. There were half a dozen boxes full of Aunt Lena's things left to put on display, so she tackled the job with even more energy than normal.

"He'll do fine," she told herself for the umpteenth time. "There's no way he won't make it through the first round." *Unless he gets a cow with a blind eye, or one that won't do anything.* "He'll probably beat everybody else by ten points. Unless he's thinkin' about us or not feeling well." *He did sound a little stuffy this morning.* "I wonder if he thought to take any decongestants with him. He didn't. I just know he didn't." She sighed. "I should have gone with him. What if he gets a cow that just runs along the fence?"

A soft chuckle behind her sent her twirling around so fast she almost fell down. Her minister was leaning against the counter with his arms crossed and a sympathetic smile on his face. She suspected he'd been standing there for several minutes. "Clint! Hello. Is the bell working? I didn't hear you come in."

"It's working. You were too busy talking to yourself." He walked over and put his arm around her shoulders in a friendly hug. "I came by to see if you'd heard from Grant. Obviously you haven't."

"He's supposed to be riding any minute now. I know he'll do fine, but I'm a nervous wreck."

"So I noticed. Dawn, even if you were there, you couldn't do a thing about it if the cow didn't cooperate," he said with a teasing smile. "He has riders in the arena to help with that job."

"I know. I just wish I'd gone, too. I should be there for him."

"You and Kim are going later aren't you?"

She nodded. "Weekend after next, for the semifinals and finals."

"Good. He'll need you more then."

"Wade and Andi are there now. They plan to stay in Fort Worth until he finishes the second go-round and comes home."

"They'll give him plenty of encouragement." Clint glanced around the store. "Think I'll wander around a bit, see if I can find something for my mom's birthday."

"Go ahead. Just ignore any muttering you hear from my direction."

"If you'll ignore mine. I tend to talk to myself, too." He disappeared behind a large bookcase.

Dawn turned back to her project, gazing at it in dismay. "Might be considered artistic if a first-grader had done it." She began rearranging the glass figurines to show the best features of each one. When the phone rang ten minutes later, she almost knocked the lot of them off in her mad dash to answer it.

"Hi, sugar. Miss me?" Grant's voice sounded warm, tender, and upbeat.

"You know I do. How was the ride?"

"Oh, I squeaked by."

"You did better than that. I can tell by your voice. What was the score?"

"Just a little ol' 220."

"Wonderful! I knew you'd do great. Breeze clear through to the finals."

Clint walked up, laughing quietly.

"Who's there?" A slight hardness crept into Grant's voice.

"Clint. He stopped by to see if I'd heard from you. Want to say hello?"

"Sure."

Dawn handed the pastor the phone. Grant and Clint had liked each other the first time they met, and they quickly became friends. They chatted for several minutes. From listening to half the conversation, Dawn gathered Grant was giving him a step-by-step account of his ride. Then she sensed Clint's gaze on her.

"Yes, your lady is still here," he said with twinkling eyes. "She hasn't moved an inch since she handed me the phone. It's a good thing you called. She was having quite a conversation with herself when I came in. I have the vague impression she was worried about you and misses you. Yes, I'll look in on her occasionally. Take care." He handed her the phone and glanced at his watch. "I have to run, but I'll be back tomorrow to look for that present. Call me if you need anything."

Dawn smiled at her friend. "I will. Thanks." She waited a few seconds, watching him walk toward the door, then lifted the receiver to her ear. "Hi there," she said softly.

Grant made a humming sound deep in his throat. "How do you do that?"

"Do what?"

"Tell me you love me just by saying hello."

"Guess it just kinda seeps through because I'm thinking it."

"Keep thinkin' it."

She heard an announcement over the loud speaker in the background and applause. Then the noise lessened slightly, as if he had shifted positions to muffle the sound.

"I love you, Dawn."

She closed her eyes, reveling in the sheer delight stirred by those precious words. "I love you, too."

"You doin' all right?"

"Fine, except I'm lonesome. I've had several buying customers today. Sold some more of Aunt Lena's stuff. If you're nice, I'll give you a big check when you come home."

"I'd rather have a big, sloppy kiss."

She laughed. "You'll get that, too. Probably several of them, but only one check. Until next month."

More noise came over the line. "I'll call you tonight from the motel. It's too hard to hear. I'm going to help Pete with his ride and another guy who asked me today. Then I'm goin' out to dinner with Andi and Wade. I'll try not to be too late."

"Call me anyway. Are you going to call Kim now?"

"Yes. I expect she and Mom have been sittin' by the phone for the last hour. She's probably chewed her fingernails down to the nubs by now. Talk to you later."

Dawn said good-bye and hung up the phone. Happiness and loneliness swirled through her. "Better get used to this, kiddo. If he does well, they'll be entering more high stakes competitions." They had talked about the possibilities if Dancer won or even placed high in the standings. If he competed for three or four more years and did very well, he could prove valuable in a breeding program. Dancer didn't have the high-class blood lines of the most expensive cutting horses, but if he had an impressive record, he could make a name for himself.

Grant called her again that night and they talked for well over an hour. He told her all about the competition, mentioning some of the people she had met at the Double L. There were so many entrants in the open category that the first go-round would last three days. The second go-round could last one or two. He intended to come home after the second go. If he made the semifinals, they would all return to Fort Worth later the following week for the rest of the competition.

Dawn went through the motions of working over the next few days, beginning to feel as if her life revolved around the telephone. Grant called several times a day, usually only talking for a few minutes, then for an hour or so at night.

Grant's turn to ride in the second level of competition didn't come until late in the evening on Thursday. When the phone rang and Dawn heard his jubilant, "Hi, sugar!" she knew he had done well. He decided not to try to drive home that night but to come home the next morning.

She hadn't been at the store fifteen minutes Friday morning when he came sauntering through the door, handsome as ever in a pine-green Western shirt and black jeans. Sweeping her up in a giant bear hug, he spun her around, then kissed her soundly. Slowly lowering her feet to the floor, he grinned and straightened his new straw hat before it fell off. "Howdy, ma'am. Mmm, you smell like fresh cantaloupe this mornin'."

"Howdy yourself. Got up with the roosters again, huh?"

He nudged his hat up on his forehead and winked. "Beat 'em up this time. I headed out about four. Would have been here sooner, but Dancer wanted biscuits and gravy for breakfast. We had to pull in at a truck stop. Dadgummed horse ate three helpings. Then Gus insisted on a piece of blueberry pie."

She laughed and squeezed him around the middle. "Feels like you're the one who's been fillin' up on blueberry pie. Here I thought you'd waste away to nothing because you were pining for me."

"Well, I tell you, I was pinin' plenty, but I figured you'd rather have me fit than scrawny. Besides, I was bored out of my gourd about half the time, so I munched."

"I'm not complaining. You look wonderful."

"So do you." He leaned down and kissed her again. "I'd much rather stay here, but I've got a couple of grumblin' horses that are past ready to get out of the trailer. And I have a heap a work waiting, so I'd better hit the trail."

"Come for dinner tonight? Lasagna."

"Sweetheart, I'd be there if you were servin' Spam."

Grant arrived at her house at six-thirty with a bouquet of carnations and a giant souvenir plastic cup from the Derby filled with chocolate kisses. They enjoyed Dawn's tossed salad, lasagna, and french bread along with quiet conversation. Dawn caught him up on the local news, and they made plans for their upcoming trip back to Fort Worth the next week. Then they cuddled on the couch and watched an old John Wayne western, sharing chocolate kisses—and real ones—for dessert.

Eighteen

On the morning of the open semifinals, Dawn met Grant at Will Rogers Coliseum at nine. He had gone to the arena earlier to prepare Dancer for the event and limber him up with a lope around the pen. She was sharing a room with Kim so Grant would be free to leave as early in the mornings as he needed. Since he was not scheduled to ride until later in the afternoon, Kim had gone with Marla Davis and her daughter to see some of the sights.

Dawn settled into the seat next to him with a smile. "Good morning, handsome."

He mumbled something that might have passed for "Mornin', sugar," but she wasn't quite sure. He was leaning forward, with his elbows on the seat back in front of him, resting his chin on his thumbs, his fingers curled up in front of his mouth. Totally focused on the rider, horse, and cow in the center of the arena, he watched every move with a critical eye and an ever-increasing frown.

Dawn turned her attention to the horse and rider. Even with her limited knowledge of the sport, it did not take the shouts of approval from the onlookers to tell her this would be a difficult ride to beat. As the seconds ticked off and the noise of the crowd increased, she watched the set of Grant's shoulders grow stiff and the muscles in his back tense. When the buzzer sounded, and the rider lifted his hand, taking the horse off the cow, most of the onlookers were on their feet.

Grant slumped back in the seat, exhaling heavily and stared at the judges lined up on the far side of the coliseum. When the scores flashed up, totaling 222, he groaned and closed his eyes.

She wrapped her hand around his. "Hey, don't worry. You did that well in the first round. You can beat him. It's a piece of cake."

He glared at her. "No ride at this level is a sure thing. That's the third score above 218 since they started at eight. At this rate, I'm liable to need a 220 to even get into the final round."

"Then you'll do it."

"I only got a 217 in the second go-round." He stared sullenly at the cutting pen as the next rider slowly moved through the herd.

"You said everyone scored lower in the second go than they did in the first."

"Well, they're not scoring low this time," he snapped.

"What made you so grumpy this morning?"

"I'm not grumpy," he growled, then looked around with a scowl. "Where's Kim?"

"She went to Old City Park in Dallas with Marla and Tiffany, remember? They're having some demonstrations, showing how folks used to churn butter and make horse shoes and other things. Marla talked to you about it last night. They'll be back after lunch."

He nodded curtly. The crowd groaned as the next rider lost his cow when the heifer raced past him back to the herd. The only indication that Grant felt anything was a twitch in his jaw.

"How's Dancer?"

"Fine."

"When did you come over here this morning?"

"Four."

"Isn't that a little early? I though most folks didn't show up until five or six."

"Couldn't sleep."

"Oh." Dawn sat quietly, silently tapping her thumbs together as she watched the preparations for the next ride. Tension radiated from the man next to her, seeping into her, heightening her already taut nerves. She wanted him to win, not only because the money would help him achieve his dream but because he needed the satisfaction of the accomplishment. He was a man who lived by the old adage, "if it's worth doing, it's worth doing well."

Failure did not come easily to anyone, but Grant had a harder time accepting it than most. She supposed it was partly due to his nature but mainly because of the experiences life had handed him. She quit tapping her fingers and started jiggling her leg.

"Will you be still!" He didn't yell, but he might as well have.

"When I'm tense, I have to move."

"Then move somewhere else. You're drivin' me up the wall. Go shopping or something."

Dawn bristled. "All right, I will. Maybe you'll decide to quit snarling by the time I get back." She stood and walked a few steps, then turned around and went back, snatching up the half-filled paper coffee cup beside his feet. "Stay away from caffeine.

And if you haven't had breakfast, go get some. You're as cranky as an old bear fresh out of hibernation." With that, she stomped off, throwing the warm coffee in the garbage can.

Halfway out of the building, regret washed over her. "Of all the days to be on his case," she muttered in disgust. Turning around she hurried back to apologize, but he was no longer sitting where he had been. She slowly looked around the bleachers but couldn't spot him. Going next door to the exhibition center, she quickly went up and down each aisle, hoping to find him at one of the booths, but he was nowhere in sight. She thought about going back to the motel but knew he wouldn't be there. He was supposed to work as a turnback man for a couple of riders during the morning.

Miserable, she drummed her fingers against her purse. "Now what? I could care less about going shopping." She glanced at her watch and decided to call Alex's store and see if he was in. He was, so she caught a taxi and went to see him.

When she walked through the doorway of his upscale antique store, he was busy with a customer. She strolled around, admiring some of the English furniture and eighteenth-century paintings he had for sale. Generally she preferred the more common, less expensive items she carried in her shop to the ornate silver tea sets and imported glassware in his.

Alex caught up with her and gave her a hug. Then he looked down and frowned. "How are you, sunshine?"

"Mad at myself. Grant was grouchy, and I ran out of patience and went off in a huff. Now I feel like a creep."

"Is he at the coliseum?" When she nodded, he continued, "Do you want to try to have him paged and talk to him? You know you can use the phone in my office."

"No, I'd probably scare him spitless if I had him paged. Kim is off on an excursion with friends, and he'd think something had happened to her. I'll just hang around here for a while and give him some space. He's supposed to help some of the other riders this morning, so maybe that will help him work off his nervousness. I was just surprised to see him so tense and irritable. He was fine last night. A little distracted, but he seemed in a good mood."

"Well, I have some news that might put him in a better frame of mind. I tried to call you yesterday to tell you, but evidently you were on your way here to the big city. Let's go to my office, and I'll tell you all about it."

Heart pounding with excitement, Dawn followed him down a long aisle and into his office. "You sold the jukebox?" she asked, as soon as he shut the door.

"Yes, ma'am. To the tune of eight thousand dollars," he said with a grin, then guided her to a chair.

"Eight thousand?" She sank onto the chair with her mouth gaping open. "I hadn't expected quite so much," she croaked.

"You heard right. I had three clients who wanted it, and two of them are old rivals of sorts. We had ourselves a little bidding war. It was great fun. And on top of that, both arcade machines sold that same morning, one for nineteen hundred, the other for two thousand." Alex walked around behind his desk and sat down in a thickly cushioned leather chair. "I can't remember when I've had such a good time in the business.

"In fact, I'm hoping you'll say you have more wonderful finds sitting out there in the middle of nowhere. They've been moving faster than anything else in the store. All I did was put out the word. I should have called you sooner, but it's been so exciting I kept waiting to see what would go next."

Dazed, she shook her head. "I brought you all the high-priced things. I've gone through all the boxes and trunks. Grant has some old ranch equipment out in the tack room, but other than a few pieces of furniture, we're not talking anything worth over five hundred."

"That's too bad, but I knew it couldn't last. These kinds of finds come along once or twice in a career, if at all. We sold several of the candy containers. The Jackie Coogan and Mr. Rabbit were the first to go at eleven hundred each, and just this morning another client—a friend of the one who bought the others—called and paid fourteen hundred for the Victory Glass Refrigerator."

"Whew! That's a little more than I thought, too. You're quite the salesman, old friend."

He winked. "Should be. Been in the business a zillion years."

Dawn laughed. They had all helped him celebrate his fiftieth birthday the day after Christmas. "You mean a zillion years' experience rolled into twenty-five. How about the prints? Are they really older reprints or was I just wishing? I keep thinking that someone must have done some clever reproductions."

A bright glimmer lit his eyes. "No, my dear, you weren't wishing. I had them checked by a noted authority. Your judgment was a little blinded by skepticism, however. The Currier and Ives are original prints, all thirty of them, published from the 1850s to the 1880s. We've sold all but three of the smaller, less valuable ones, and I expect they will go shortly. Most of the prints were in the two to five hundred dollar range, but three proved to be far more valuable than I first thought. *The Old Homestead in Winter*, 1864, went for eight thousand dollars."

"Alex, you can't be serious!" Dawn jumped up from her chair and began to pace.

He threw back his head and laughed. "I'm very serious. And I've saved the best for last. Maybe you'd better sit down while I tell you the rest."

"Can't." She continued to pace, walking quicker. "I have to keep moving. Tell me fast."

"*Husking,* dated 1861, sold for ninety-five hundred." He paused, and Dawn stopped and held her breath. "And the *American National Game of Baseball,* dated 1866, sold for twenty-five thousand dollars yesterday."

She sank to a sitting position on the floor. Alex jumped up, running around the desk, and kneeled beside her. "Put your head down."

She shook it instead. "No, I'm all right. Just stunned. I promise I won't faint or throw up." She looked up at him. "I'm afraid to ask about the Audubons."

He took hold of her elbow and pulled her to her feet, shoving a chair behind her, then hung onto her arm until she sat down. Leaning against his desk, he grinned cheekily. "Want to know about the birds, huh? Well, you were partly right on those. Some were reprints done in the middle of the last century, and even those were worth a pretty penny. The least valuable one went for two thousand. Four of the prints have proven to be originals."

Dawn gasped and put her hand over her mouth.

"It seems some originals are more valuable than others, depending on the print. Two of them went for seven thousand five hundred each. The last two went for considerably more. *Whooping Crane* sold for twenty thousand, and the Trumpeter Swan went for thirty...thousand."

Dawn bent over and put her head between her knees.

Alex instantly knelt beside her. "Okay, sunshine?" He laughed when she wiggled her head. "I can't tell if that's a yes or a no."

"It's a yes. Just give me a minute."

"And a check?"

"Checks are nice." She sat up slowly and smiled, trying to assimilate everything he had told her. "Some checks are very nice."

He walked back around his desk. "I think this time sending the money electronically from my bank to yours would be the best way to handle it. I'll get the exact figures from my bookkeeper and ask her to handle it while I take you out to lunch, then give you a ride back to the coliseum."

She nodded. "Except, this time lunch is on me. Pick your favorite place, and I don't care how fancy."

Hands beneath his head, Grant lay stretched out on the bed staring at the ceiling of the motel room. He'd come back to his room hoping to rest, but sleep had been as elusive after lunch as it had been during the night. Glancing at the clock, he rolled over on his side and swung his legs over the edge of the bed, sitting up. "We have to place in the money. I can't let my girls down."

As he pulled on his boots, his mind ran over the list of his failures, starting when he was a kid, going through the times he hadn't given Susan what she needed or wanted, through every little stupid mistake or dumb thing he had said or done with Dawn, up to the way he had treated her that morning.

Buying back the rest of the ranch was no longer a high priority.

Making a good living for Dawn and Kim was at the top of his list. *No, I want better than good.* He wouldn't let them down the way he had Susan. The ranch would provide their basic needs and even other things—in a good year. But what if more children came along? What would he do when his old pickup finally rolled over and died? Or that ancient tractor quit running? He could think of dozens of things that would take extra money—and plenty of it.

"If Dancer can win, and keep winning, we'll do all right. In three or four years we can start a breeding program, and that will carry us on for a while longer. If we don't win, I don't know what I'll do." *So much can go wrong. I can mess it all up so easy.*

He walked over and picked up his shirt from the chair, putting it on. He glanced at the clock again. "Where is she? I've got to see her before I ride. Apologize for this mornin'. Feel her lovin' arms around me and see the forgiveness in her eyes." He listened, hoping to hear movement in the adjoining room, but there was no sound to indicate Dawn had returned.

Walking over to the window, he fastened the snaps on his shirt and absently looked down at the parking lot two floors below. A white Lincoln pulled up in a vacant space across from the stairs, and a handsome, distinguished looking man climbed out. Grant frowned, watching him walk around the back of the car to the other side. "That's no cowboy, and I'll waltz with a catfish if he's a rancher." He figured the man was about forty-five, but he was in good shape, and he had money written all over him.

Grant froze when the man opened the car door and extended his hand, assisting a pretty, young blonde from the Lincoln. *Dawn.* "What's she doin' with that guy! Some shopping trip," he cried angrily, noting the brightly wrapped package in her hand.

Then, without a thought or care who might see them, they embraced right there in the parking lot. Grant clenched his fists and pounded them against the window sill, but like a fly caught in a spider web, he stood transfixed, unable to move or look away. They drew apart. The stranger said something and she laughed, then raised up on tiptoe and kissed his cheek.

Grant went ballistic. Bolting back from the window, he stuffed his shirttail in his pants and stalked over to the door connecting their rooms, turning the lock so hard it almost broke. He automatically put on his belt and watch, mumbling vehemently about unfaithful women and fools who believed in them. His mind teemed with ways to squash slick, city fat cats who paraded around in fancy cars and showered gifts on women, stealing them away from their men.

He was stuffing his wallet in his hip pocket when a knock sounded on the door, a distinctive little pattern of taps that he instantly recognized. *Dawn. Of all the nerve!* Shocked by her audacity, he held his breath as she knocked again. He couldn't face her now, couldn't let her see his pain. If he opened the door, he was liable to pick her up and shake her like a rag doll.

She quit knocking, and he listened as the door to the next room opened and closed. He heard her purse land on the dresser beside the connecting door, then the radio came on to a country station, and she sang along, happy as a lark.

He thought he might die from the pain.

Walking quietly into the bathroom, he splashed cold water on his face and dried it. Looking into the mirror, he saw the reflection of a broken man. Slowly, he straightened. Picking up his comb, he methodically ran it through his hair. He checked his belt, centering the buckle slightly, and fastened the snaps on his shirt sleeves.

He walked back into the bedroom and picked up his hat, setting it carefully on his head. Squaring his shoulders, he met the cold, hard gaze staring back at him in the dresser mirror. "Twice the fool, but never again."

Nineteen

❧

W hen Dawn arrived at Will Rogers Coliseum and found Marla and her daughter with Kim in the grandstands, she learned Grant would be riding sooner than scheduled.

"One rider had a family emergency and had to leave. Another one's horse got sick. Pete says it looks like blister beetle poisoning."

"What's that? It sounds terrible."

"Sometimes blister beetles will invade fields of alfalfa. If the hay is harvested with the beetle infestation, when the beetles die, they secrete a poison that is toxic to horses. Sometimes they can save them, but not always."

"Are any of the other horses sick?" Dawn thought how badly it would hurt Grant if he lost Dancer or Gus, how badly it would hurt them all.

"No, they think it was an isolated bale. Kind of a freakish thing. Pete said the horse must not have liked the taste because she didn't eat much of it. The vet says she should pull through."

"Well, that's a relief." Dawn reached over and hugged Kim.

"How you doin', punkin? Did you have fun today?"

"It was great. We saw a lady churn butter by moving this stick up and down inside a big crock. She was wearing an old-fashioned dress and had her hair pulled back in a bun. She was real funny, told us all the gossip about her pretend neighbors. There was all sorts of fun stuff to see." Kim frowned. "Have you talked to Daddy lately?"

"No. He was crabby this morning and got mad at me. I got angry, too, and left, which was a stupid thing to do. I came back looking for him, but I couldn't find him. So I went to visit my friend Alex at his antique store. Did you see your daddy? How's he doing?"

"Not good. I don't know what's wrong, but he's mad as a rained-on rooster. He didn't yell at me. He didn't hardly say nothin'."

"Oh, dear. I'd better go find him and apologize. It's all my fault. I should have been more patient. I never should have left. Do you know where he is?" She glanced at Marla.

"He's getting ready to ride. There are only two more before him. He sure needs consolin' about something. He's cold on the outside, but seething on the inside. Pete said he'd try to find out what's wrong, see if he can get him to talk it out. He's in for a bad ride if he can't."

Dawn raced down the aisle and ran all the way to the area where the horses and riders waited their turn. Grant was about to mount up when she found him. "I'm so glad I caught you," she said breathlessly, laying her hand on his arm.

He looked down at her hand, then slowly lifted his gaze. She stepped back, shocked by his hard expression and the rage burning in his eyes. "Why on earth should you care if you saw me or not?"

"Because I love you!"

"Right. And pigs fly."

"Grant, I'm sorry I got mad at you this morning. I know you're under a lot of strain, and I should have been more understanding. I should have stayed here, been here for you."

He kept one hand on the saddle horn, the other on the cantle. "What makes you think I want you around?" he ground out in a low voice. "I didn't want you here this morning, and I don't want you here now."

Stunned, Dawn could only watch as he swung up into the saddle and carefully guided Dancer away, threading expertly through the maze of horses and riders.

Pete walked up next to her, leading his horse. "I don't know what's ailin' him. Somethin's stuck in his craw, and he's gonna choke on it if he ain't careful."

"I know I let him down this morning, but he can't be this angry because we had a silly spat. Oh, Pete, try to talk to him!"

"I already tried and he ain't talkin'. He's not listening right now, either. I'll help him as much as I can on this ride, but you'd better send up some arrow prayers real quick 'cause the kind of help he needs, I can't give. I don't think this has to do with this morning. He mentioned at lunch that he needed to see you so he could apologize." Pete mounted his horse. "Even went back to the motel, hoping to catch a little shut-eye and talk to you. We'll see you later. I hope." He turned his horse away and followed Grant toward the loping pen.

Dawn walked back toward the grandstands, dodging people and horses. Once she was free of the staging area, she could concentrate on what had happened with Grant and what Pete had said. She walked through the crowd, running it all through her mind. *He went back to the motel. Wanted to apologize and get some rest. After lunch.* "After lunch!" she exclaimed, drawing odd looks from a couple passing by. *He must have seen Alex bring me back.*

She tried to remember what had happened when Alex dropped her off. They were excited and speculating on Grant's reaction when he found out how much money he had coming. He'd hugged her and she'd kissed him on the cheek with affection and gratitude. She pictured the scene the way Grant must have seen it and dismay swept through her. Given his state of mind at the time, and the fact that he was still working through the hurts of the past—hurts that seemed to keep breeding distrust—he could have concluded only one thing.

Father, help him to think rationally. Make him realize who I was with. Sadly, she knew Grant had no reason to think she was with Alex. He'd never seen the man. As far as he knew, she'd gone shopping. Walking to her seat, Dawn prayed silently but fervently. *Lord, calm him down. Give him peace, if only for the ride. Please let them do their best.*

When she sat down next to Kim, the girl looked up with worried eyes. "Pray for him, honey. He misunderstood something that happened today, and he's really upset. I didn't have the chance to explain, so we're going to have to pray him through the ride."

"Okay. He's up next." Kim turned back toward the arena, never taking her gaze off her dad.

Dawn glanced at the girl's clenched hands and knew Kim was praying with every bit of faith she possessed. She did the same.

Grant went into the herd a little too fast, but Dancer seemed to realize it and slowed his pace. They moved deep into the middle of the herd—one of the requirements of the competition was making a deep cut—and drove out six or seven cattle. Grant picked out a Hereford, carefully separated her away from the others, drove her toward the center of the arena, and dropped his rein hand down in front of the saddle. The cow seemed nonchalant, almost bored with the whole thing. "Oh, no, he picked a dud," she whispered.

For a few seconds—that seemed like hours—the cow stood staring at them. Dancer quivered with energy and excitement. He took a little half-step toward the cow, issuing a challenge, and the Hereford took off like a shot. Dancer kept up every step of the way, blocking her path with a deep, skidding halt. The cow headed back the other way, but this time the horse almost ran past her when she stopped.

"Slump, Daddy!" screamed Kim. "Slump!"

At Kim's cry, Dawn realized that Grant was tense and sitting up too straight, which hampered his ability to move with the horse. A good rider assumed what was called the cutter's slump, with lower back and hips relaxed. Grant had said a good way to think of it was to remember to sit on his back pockets. Suddenly, as if he had heard Kim's shrill plea, he shifted slightly, bending his back, and slumped down in the saddle. Tears stung her eyes.

They made some good moves, blocking the cow each time, then suddenly she raised her head, spun around and ran directly away from them toward the other end of the arena. Grant raised his hand, signaling that he was quitting the cow. He straightened out the reins and turned Dancer back toward the herd.

They didn't go as deeply into the herd this time but drove out three cows, again without disturbing the others. Two of the cattle moved off together to one side, and Grant and Dancer went to work with the third. This one didn't give them quite as good a run as the first one, but they didn't make any mistakes that Dawn could see.

When the scores were tallied, he came up with 216. Dawn looked over Kim's head at Marla. "Is that good enough to go to the finals?"

"Maybe. Pete said there were some high scores earlier today, but there's been a real streak of low ones. I think there are about six riders left to go."

It seemed an eternity until Grant came walking up the bleacher steps. She figured he had taken care of Dancer and returned him to his stall before coming up to sit with them. Only one rider remained, and even if he scored high, Grant was already assured of a place in the final round. When Kim spotted him, she jumped up and raced down to meet him, giving him a big hug.

He smiled and accepted her praise with grace, but Dawn could see he wasn't a happy man. When he and Kim walked down their row of seats, he planted his daughter between him and Dawn.

"Congratulations." She smiled, but it was forced, and she knew he could tell.

He nodded curtly, accepting Marla's praise with only slightly more enthusiasm. "Should have ridden better. Lucky I made the cut."

"It wasn't luck, Daddy. We were prayin' really hard for you. Did you hear me tell you to slump?"

A tiny smile touched his face, chasing away some of the turbulence in his eyes. "Yes, punkin', I did. Thank you. I was stiff as a board, and we probably wouldn't have made it without your advice."

"I didn't think you would hear me since everybody else was yelling, too."

He put his arm around her. "It was the daddy part that did it. Guess my ears are tuned to that particular word."

Kim giggled and looked up at him in adoration. He smiled down at her, then raised his gaze to lock with Dawn's. His smile faded and anger surged through his eyes. He glanced back down at his daughter. "I'm plumb tuckered out. You ready to go back to the motel?"

"Sure." As he stood, Kim hopped up and held out her hand to Dawn. "Come on."

Dawn hesitated, meeting Grant's gaze. For an awful moment she thought he was going to tell her to find her own way back to the motel. Then he gave her a short nod and turned away.

As if sensing the tension between them on the way back to the motel, Kim prattled on and on about her trip to Old City Park in Dallas. Dawn barely heard what she was saying. Judging from Grant's sometimes inappropriate comments, he wasn't doing any better.

Once inside their rooms, Dawn sat down next to Kim on one of the queen-sized beds. "I need to talk to your daddy. Do you need anything before I try to corner him?"

"Let me run down the hall and get some ice for my pop. I'll be right back." She grabbed the ice bucket and went out the door. Three minutes later she knocked, and Dawn let her in.

Dawn took a deep breath and knocked on the door connecting their room with Grant's. Watching Kim pour a Dr. Pepper over ice in a motel glass, she had almost decided he wasn't going to answer the door, when it flew open. "We need to talk," she said quietly.

"There's no way you can talk yourself out of this one." Anger lurked beneath the surface of his tired expression and voice.

"I think there is. Please, let me explain." When he looked as if he might shut the door in her face, she crossed her arms and defiantly tipped up her chin. "I'll stand here and pound on this door all night if I have to, so you might as well hear me out now."

"Stubborn woman." He stepped back with a glare, closing the door behind her when she walked into the room. "Make it quick. I'm tired."

"All right. First of all, this isn't about me leaving this morning, is it?"

He shook his head and crossed his arms, leaning against the door. "No, I was the one in the wrong there."

"We both were. I shouldn't have left."

"But you did and very conveniently found more pleasant company."

She wandered around the room. Sitting or standing still was an impossibility. "I went to see Alex at his store. Then we went out to lunch, and he brought me back to the motel."

Grant lowered his arms and moved toward her, stopping a few feet away. One hand curled into a fist, then opened. "I must be getting slow. When you said Alex was a close friend, I didn't catch exactly what you meant. Just how long has this *friendship* been going on?"

"Since I was born. Alex and Rita are my godparents. Their youngest daughter is named after me. He is a wonderful Christian man who has been happily married for twenty-nine years. He loves his wife deeply, and I have no doubts whatsoever that he has been faithful to her every minute of that time."

She slowly approached him, watching uncertainty war with disbelief on his face. "Grant, I know you probably saw me hug him and give him a kiss on the cheek, but it was all innocent. I love him, but like an uncle."

Taking heart when he didn't deny her statement or turn away, she stopped in front of him and slid her arms around his neck. "I know you were upset today and not seeing things in a clear light, but please get this through your gorgeous, hard head—I'm not Susan. I'll never be like her. I'm a one-man woman. Period. Grant, I love you. Only you. I love you with all my heart and soul, and nothing—not even you—will ever make me stop loving you."

He dropped down on the edge of the bed, pulling her down to sit on his lap. He closed his eyes and groaned. "I'm an idiot."

She nodded. "On rare occasions, but I love you anyway."

"I sure don't know why." He met her gaze, his expression filled with regret and worry.

"Because being with you fills me with happiness," she said softly, "and having your arms around me makes my heart sing. Your joy is my joy; your sorrow, my sorrow. You laugh with me but also understand my fears. You give me strength when I feel weak, yet you need me. But most of all, I love you because God saw two lonely hearts and made them beat as one. You are his gift to me, just as I am his gift to you."

"And I'll thank him all my days," he whispered, kissing her with love and passion, seeking forgiveness for his lack of trust and the hurt he had caused her. He buried his face against the side of her neck, holding her as tight as he dared. "Forgive me, please. When I thought I'd lost you…" His voice trailed off, and he took a deep, shuddering breath. "I love you more than I ever thought I could love anyone. I don't want to lose you."

She kissed his forehead. "You're not going to. Whether you want me to or not, I intend to hang around and joyfully drive you crazy."

He raised his head and saw the promise of forever in her eyes. This beautiful miracle loved him—she truly loved him. In spite of his mistakes, his insecurities, his failures, she loved him and would be faithful until the end of time. He wanted to laugh and cry and sing and shout—maybe even dance like Fred Astaire. "I want you around forever, although I'd just as soon you didn't drive me crazy in the process. I need you and your love to give me strength and joy and brighten my heart." He gently framed her face with his hands. "Dawn Carson, love of my life, will you marry me?"

"Didn't I already say yes to that?" she asked him with a grin. "Yes, my love, I'll marry you." Then she kissed him, taking her time and putting plenty of effort into it. He feathered tiny kisses over her face, murmuring words of love. Several minutes later, she smiled and moved off his lap to sit next to him. "I don't want to hurt that knee before you can walk down the aisle."

He shrugged aside her worry, dealing with a bigger one of his own. "I'll try my best to provide a good living for you, although if I don't win the Derby, I'm not sure how well we'll do."

She frowned. "Is that what was bothering you this morning?"

He nodded, wanting her to understand how much it meant to him to give her a good life. "I don't care about buying any more land, but I want to give you the things you need. I want to be able to buy you nice clothes and a new pickup and take you on a cruise if you want. I want Kim to go to college. I don't want to let you and Kim down."

"Grant, you aren't going to let us down, even if you don't win. We'll be just as proud of you and love you just as much if you come in last. Besides, I get seasick in a rowboat. Believe me, I will never want to take a cruise. Yes, you need a new pickup, but it will be a few years before Kim is ready for college. I have no intention of giving up my antique business, so I can buy my own clothes. In fact, we can go buy a new pickup right now if you want."

"I'm not going to spend your money on a new pickup," he said with a stubborn frown.

"Then spend yours."

"I earned some in the first and second go-rounds, but I haven't won near that much."

"Pocket change. I haven't had a chance to tell you what Alex and I were so happy and excited about."

Grant noted the new sparkle that came into her eyes. Not as brilliant as the stars his marriage proposal had induced, but it was an intriguing twinkle just the same. "He sold some of Aunt Lena's stuff?"

"A great deal of Aunt Lena's stuff, and some of it proved to be far more valuable than even I—with all my astute knowledge of the business—had expected. He transferred the funds to the bank in Buckley this afternoon."

Grant narrowed his eyes, trying to decide if she was teasing him. "How much?"

"Well…after Alex took out his commission, your half is $41,491.48."

His mouth fell open. He snapped it shut and stood carefully. "Say that again."

"Nope. Too much trouble. Of course, since we're going to be married, my half will go into the family kitty, too, which gives us eighty-two thousand, nine hundred and some odd dollars. I spent some already. And he still has a few of the lesser items to sell. So, I think we can afford a new pickup. Even a hot tub."

"A new pickup and a hot tub," he mumbled in disbelief. He thought of all the nights he came in with his knee aching and the rest of his body tired and sore from hard physical labor. *How did she guess how much he wanted a hot tub?* "A hot tub!" He cut loose with a Rebel yell and grabbed her up in a giant hug. He was considering kissing the woman senseless when Kim burst into the room.

"Daddy, what's going on?"

He set Dawn's feet on the ground and held her close to his side. "Well, for starters, this beautiful, wonderful woman has agreed to marry me."

"Hey, all right!" Kim raced over and threw her arms around them both. "Can I call you Mom?"

Grant watched tears well up in Dawn's eyes as she held his daughter—their daughter—close.

"Honey, I'd be honored for you to call me Mom, Mama, or anything else you want to."

"Cool!" Kim stepped back. "What else?"

"Dawn's friend, Alex, has sold some of Aunt Lena's collectibles, and we made a bundle. We're thinkin' about buying a new pickup. And maybe a hot tub."

"And probably a few acres of land, too," said Dawn, squeezing him around the middle.

"All right! Can I have a phone in my room?"

Grant looked at Dawn, then back at Kim. "Uh, aren't you a little young for that?"

"Aw, Dad, I won't be talking to boys." She grinned. "But my friends and I might want to talk about them, and I'd rather not do that with you hanging around." She glanced at Dawn and smiled. "Or Mom, either."

"I don't think she's too young for a phone," said Dawn. "She can use it to study with her friends."

"Something tells me I'm going to be outnumbered in my own home."

"And you're gonna love it." Dawn stretched up and kissed him.

"Yes, ma'am. I do believe I am. Did you say something about a present?"

"Coming right up." She scampered into her room and returned with the brightly wrapped package he had seen her carrying earlier. "I couldn't resist it when I spotted it."

He sat down on the bed and tore off the paper like a kid at Christmas. When he opened the box, he found a book of photographs portraying life on the Texas range around the turn of the century. He'd never seen any better ones. "This is great. We can leave it out on the coffee table for everybody to see." He stood and held her close. "Thank you."

"You're welcome. I figured your great-grandpa and grandpa experienced many of the same things."

"Anybody ever tell you that you're sweet?"

"Occasionally, but feel free to mention it anytime."

He laughed. "Yes, ma'am. Now, let's go call everybody we know and tell them to start gettin' ready for a wedding." He looked down at Dawn. "I'm all for copyin' your cousin and get-tin' married in a week."

"Next Saturday it is, whether anybody can come or not."

Grant was the last rider in the final round. By the time he and Dancer were poised outside the arena gate, Dawn had chewed all but one of her fingernails down to the quick. The announcer pointed out the rarity of a non-professional making it this far in the competition. He shared the story of how Grant had rescued Dancer from probable death, brought him back to good health, and discovered a natural-born cutting horse.

Off went the last fingernail.

"This is a horse with a great big heart and a lot of cow. He loves keepin' those critters in line. They had a little trouble in the semifinals and just squeaked by, but Grant confided earlier that it was all his fault because he was worryin' too much. They won't have that problem tonight, folks. The man is so happy he's prac-tically floatin' on the saddle. He told me he proposed last night to the sweetest little lady in the whole wide world, and she said yes."

The crowd clapped, whistled, and cheered. Dawn grinned and turned scarlet, but she didn't care. She was also floating on air, even if she ached to see Grant win. He looked straight up at her and smiled, touching the brim of his hat. For a heartbeat, only the two of them existed.

Then he relaxed into the cutter's slump and a cowboy opened the gate for him. The announcer reminded the crowd that the highest score so far was 224, held by none other than Grant's good friend—and the man who had taught both him and

Dancer—Pete Davis. Beating that score would be phenomenal. The announcer pointed out that Pete was working as one of Grant's herd holders and that Grant had helped him on his run. "That's the way it is in cutting, folks. Everybody helps everybody else and does their best to give them a good run."

Grant slowly rode deep into the herd, driving out eight or nine head of cattle. As they flowed back around him, Dawn saw that he had picked a mixed breed with some Brahma in her. That type of cow could give him a good run or she could mean trouble. She held her breath and her knuckles turned white as she gripped the arms of her chair.

He eased the cow from the herd as if he had all the time in the world. Waiting until she came to a complete stop and Dancer was positioned correctly, he lowered his rein hand. Once again, Dancer took a tiny step toward the cow and the race was on. The crowd came to their feet as Dancer anticipated the cow's every move, blocking every run with sure turns, quick pivots, and deep stops. As everyone around her screamed, Dawn tried to remember to breathe.

The cow finally came to a complete stop. Grant waited a few seconds, and when she didn't move, he lifted his rein hand, signaling that he was going to another cow. He and Dancer moved into the herd, peeling off a Hereford from the outside of the group. Beside her, Dawn heard Marla murmur that he'd chosen well. That particular cow hadn't been worked so far.

Dawn was certain the clock was stuck. Never had a run seemed longer.

It was a beautiful run, even better than the first calf. Neither man nor horse made any mistakes. Dancer's moves were strong and decisive, graceful and precise. Grant seemed to be simply an extension of the horse, flowing with every movement, no matter how sudden or sharp.

With two seconds to go, the cow and Dancer stopped and faced each other. Dancer quivered with anticipation and dropped down on his knees, bringing him down to eye level with the cow. Mesmerized, the heifer stared at the masterful beast in front of her and shuddered. The buzzer sounded, ending their two-and-a-half-minute shot at glory, and the crowd roared as Grant calmly reached down and patted Dancer on the neck, taking him off the cow.

Dancer pranced out of the arena, cocky and sure of himself. Dawn could have sworn that horse was grinning almost as much as his rider. She laughed and cried, hugging Kim and Marla and the big, brawny stranger next to her. Then she clasped her hands and stared numbly at the judges. One by one the scores came up, the noise of the crowd growing with each new number until the total hit the board.

"224!" screamed the announcer. "They're tied for first place!"

Dawn and Marla shrieked and hugged each other again. Dawn hugged Kim, lifting her off the ground, then grabbed her hand and tore off down the stairs toward the arena. Marla and her daughters were right behind them. When they reached Pete and Grant, both men swept their ladies up in an embrace.

When Grant set Dawn on the ground, she framed his face with her hands. "I knew you'd do it!"

He laughed. "I knew it was a good ride, but I would've been happy with second." He gave her a quick kiss, then picked Kim up, giving her a bear hug.

"You were super, Daddy! I've never seen you ride so good."

He smiled and met Dawn's gaze. "That's because I've never

been so happy." He held Kim next to Dancer so she could give him a hug, too, then set her feet on the ground.

The announcer and several officials of the National Cutting Horse Association escorted them all to the center of the arena and presented Grant and Pete with their trophies and checks. Holding Marla's hand and his horse's reins in one hand, Pete made a little speech about the excitement of riding a good horse, the high level of competition, and the benefit of having a wife who loved him and cutting.

The announcer turned to Grant. "Well, you've had quite a weekend," he said with a big grin.

With the trophy in one hand, his other arm around Dawn, Kim standing in front of him, and Dancer reaching over his shoulder trying to get a sugar cube out of his pocket, Grant laughed. "Yes, sir. The Lord has truly blessed me, and I'm very grateful." He looked down at Dawn. "But next weekend will be even better because this wonderful woman is going to be my bride."

Kim glanced up and moved out of the way as Grant took Dawn in his arms—trophy, checks, and all—and kissed her thoroughly to the applause of several thousand happy spectators. Dancer, however, was determined to have his treat and kept nudging his shoulder. Finally, the horse hooked his nose under the side of Grant's hat and flipped it off, much to the amusement of those watching.

Without breaking the kiss, Grant shifted Dawn to one side and dug the sugar cubes out of his pocket, holding them out to Dancer in his open palm. When he finally raised his head, Dawn smiled first at him, then the horse.

"I don't care if he is a champion, he still has to sleep in the stables."

"Yes, ma'am."

After receiving dozens of congratulations, handshakes, and pats on the back—and neck in Dancer's case—they started toward the stables. Dawn looked up at the love of her life and patted the twenty-five-thousand-dollar check in his shirt pocket. "So, where do you want to go on a honeymoon?"

"Haven't thought about it. Want to do the islands like Andi and Grant?"

She shook her head. "Too hot now. I was thinking North Carolina would be nice."

He glanced down at her, then looked again. "You've got a gleam in your eye, little one. Why North Carolina?"

Dawn stepped in front of him, walking backward and talking fast. "I've heard about this wonderful antique auction every Friday night. Everything there is fresh."

He gently drew her back around to his side. "Walk over here so I won't step on you. What does fresh mean?"

"It means stuff that's never been in stores. It's straight out of homes or attics or barns...or maybe bunkhouses, if they have them in that part of the country. They have some real finds, I'm told. Ever been to an auction?"

"Yep. Go to the one in Buckley on a regular basis."

She sighed heavily, then grinned. "Not a cow auction, an antique auction."

"Can't say that I have." He draped his arm across her shoulders. "But something tells me I'll be going to one very soon."

"They're great fun. You'll love every minute of it."

He rested his face against her hair. "I know I will, sweetheart, as long as I'm with you."

Dear Reader:

When Grant first popped onto the computer screen in my previous Palisades Book, *Love Song,* I knew instantly that he was a man sorely in need of God. He also needed a loving Christian woman with a heart the size of Texas. Dawn was perfect for him, and I figured he was enough of a challenge to keep her happy and on her toes.

Like Dawn, I love old things and can spend hours browsing through antique stores, often trying to picture those who owned both common items and the unusual. I often wind up bringing something home, but the things I treasure the most are the odds and ends that have been handed down to us through the family. When I hear the steady tick and the tinny chime of my great-grandmother's clock, I'm reminded of loved ones who listened to that familiar sound as they went about their daily chores. Sometimes it's good to hold onto the past.

Sometimes, it's not. As in Grant's case, we can be worn down by life, a little frayed around the edges. There are times when we need to let go of the past and let the love of Jesus heal the hurts and make us new creatures in him. I hope you caught a glimpse of that love in *Antiques.*

May God bless each of you, and may you dwell in his love,

Sharon Gillenwater
c/o Palisades
P.O. Box 1720
Sisters, Oregon 97759

Palisades…Pure Romance

Refuge, Lisa Tawn Bergren
Torchlight, Lisa Tawn Bergren
Treasure, Lisa Tawn Bergren
Secrets, Robin Jones Gunn
Sierra, Shari MacDonald
Westward, Amanda MacLean
Glory, Marilyn Kok
Love Song, Sharon Gillenwater
Cherish, Constance Colson
Whispers, Robin Jones Gunn
Angel Valley, Peggy Darty
Stonehaven, Amanda MacLean
Antiques, Sharon Gillenwater
A Christmas Joy, Darty, Gillenwater, MacLean (October)

Titles and dates are subject to change.

Treasure, Lisa Tawn Bergren
ISBN 0-88070-725-9
She arrived on the Caribbean island of Robert's Foe armed with a lifelong
dream—to find her ancestor's sunken ship—and yet the only man who can help
her stands stubbornly in her way. Can Christina and Mitch find their way to the
ship *and* to each other?

Secrets, Robin Jones Gunn
ISBN 0-88070-721-6
Seeking a new life as an English teacher in a peaceful Oregon town, Jessica tries
desperately to hide the details of her identity from the community...until she falls
in love. Will the past keep Jessica and Kyle apart forever?

Sierra, Shari MacDonald
ISBN 0-88070-726-7
When spirited photographer Celia Randall travels to eastern California for a
short-term assignment, she quickly is drawn to—and locks horns with—editor
Marcus Stratton. Will lingering heartaches destroy Celia's chance at true love? Or
can she find hope and healing high in the *Sierra*?

Westward, Amanda MacLean
ISBN 0-88070-751-8
Running from a desperate fate in the South toward an unknown future in the
West, plantation-born artist Juliana St. Clair finds herself torn between two men,
one an undercover agent with a heart of gold, the other a man with evil inten-
tions and a smooth facade. Witness Juliana's dangerous travels toward faith and
love as she follows God's lead in this powerful historical novel.

Glory, Marilyn Kok
ISBN 0-88070-754-2
To Mariel Forrest, the teaching position in Taiwan provided more than a simple
escape from grief; it also offered an opportunity to deal with her feelings toward
the God she once loved, but ultimately blamed for the deaths of her family. Once
there, Mariel dares to ask the timeless question: "If God is good, why do we suf-
fer?" What follows is an inspiring story of love, healing, and renewed confidence
in God's goodness.

Love Song, Sharon Gillenwater
ISBN 0-88070-747-X
When famous country singer Andrea Carson returns to her hometown to recu-
perate from a life-threatening illness, she seeks nothing more than a respite from

the demands of stardom that have sapped her creativity and ability to perform. It's Andi's old high school friend Wade Jamison who helps her to realize that she needs inner healing as well. As Andi's strength grows, so do her feelings for the rancher who has captured her heart. But can their relationship withstand the demands of her career? Or will their romance be as fleeting as a beautiful *Love Song*?

Cherish, Constance Colson
ISBN 0-88070-802-6
Recovering from the heartbreak of a failed engagement, Rose Anson seeks refuge at a resort on Singing Pines Island, where she plans to spend a peaceful summer studying and painting the spectacular scenery of international Lake of the Woods. But when a flamboyant Canadian and a big-hearted American compete for her love, the young artist must face her past—and her future. What follows is a search for the source and meaning of true love: a journey that begins in the heart and concludes in the soul.

Whispers, Robin Jones Gunn
ISBN 0-88070-755-0
Teri Moreno went to Maui eager to rekindle a romance. But when circumstances turn out to be quite different than she expects, she finds herself spending a great deal of time with a handsome, old high school crush who now works at a local resort. But the situation becomes more complicated when Teri meets Gordon, a clumsy, endearing Australian with a wild past, and both men begin to pursue her. Will Teri respond to God's gentle urgings toward true love? The answer lies in her response to the gentle *Whispers* in her heart.

Angel Valley, Peggy Darty (July)
ISBN 0-88070-778-X
When teacher Laurel Hollingsworth accepts a summer tutoring position for a wealthy socialite family, she faces an enormous challenge in her young student, Anna Lisa Wentworth. However, the real challenge is ahead of her: hanging on to her heart when older brother Matthew Wentworth comes to visit. Soon Laurel and Matthew find that they share a faith in God...and powerful feelings for one another. Can Laurel and Matthew find time to explore their relationship while she helps the emotionally troubled Anna Lisa and fights to defend her love for the beautiful *Angel Valley*?

Stonehaven, Amanda MacLean (August)
ISBN 0-88070-757-7
Picking up in the years following *Westward*, *Stonehaven* follows Callie St. Clair back to the South where she has returned to reclaim her ancestral home. As she works to win back the plantation, the beautiful and dauntless Callie turns it into a station on the Underground Railroad. Covering her actions by playing the role

of a Southern belle, Callie risks losing Hawk, the only man she has ever loved. Readers will find themselves quickly drawn into this fast-paced novel of treachery, intrigue, spiritual discovery, and unexpected love.

Antiques, Sharon Gillenwater (September)
ISBN 0-88070-801-8
Deeply wounded by the infidelity of his wife, widower Grant Adams swore off all women—until meeting charming antiques dealer Dawn Carson. Although he is drawn to her, Grant struggles to trust again. Dawn finds herself overwhelmingly attracted to the darkly brooding cowboy, but won't marry a non-believer. As Grant learns more about her faith, he is touched by its impact on her life and finally accepts Christ, and together they work through Grant's inability to trust.

A Christmas Joy, MacLean, Darty, Gillenwater (October)
ISBN 0-88070-780-1 (same length as other Palisades books)
Snow falls, hearts change, and love prevails! In this compilation, three experienced Palisades authors spin three separate novelettes centering around the Christmas season and message:
By Amanda MacLean: A Christmas pageant coordinator in a remote mountain village of Northern California meets a spirited concert pianist.
By Peggy Darty: A college skiclub reunion brings together model Heather Grant and an old flame. Will they gain a new understanding?
By Sharon Gillenwater: A chance meeting in an airport that neither of them could forget...and a Christmas reunion.

PALISADES BACKLIST

Refuge, Lisa Tawn Bergren
ISBN 0-88070-621-X
Part One: A Montana rancher and a San Francisco marketing exec—only one incredible summer and God could bring such diverse lives together. *Part Two:* Lost and alone, Emily Walker needs and wants a new home, a sense of family. Can one man lead her to the greatest Father she could ever want and a life full of love?

Torchlight, Lisa Tawn Bergren
ISBN 0-88070-806-9
When beautiful heiress Julia Rierdon returns to Maine to remodel her family's estate, she finds herself torn between the man she plans to marry and unexpected feelings for a mysterious wanderer who threatens to steal her heart.

NOTE TO DEALER: CUSTOMER SHOULD PROVIDE 6 COUPONS AND YOU SHOULD RETAIN THE COUPON FROM THE FREE BOOK (#7). WE WILL SEND YOU A REPLACEMENT COPY OF THE PALISADES NOVEL YOU GIVE AWAY VIA SPRING ARBOR, CONSOLIDATED FREIGHT. (IN CANADA, CONTACT BEACON DISTRIBUTING.)

PLEASE FILL OUT:
(ON PAGE FROM FREE BOOK ONLY)

FREE BOOK TITLE _____

ISBN _____

STORE NAME _____

ADDRESS _____

_____

SPRING ARBOR CUSTOMER ID# _____
(VERY IMPORTANT!)

BEACON DISTRIBUTING ACCOUNT # (CANADIANS ONLY) _____

STAPLE THE 6 COUPONS TOGETHER WITH #7 AND THE INFORMATION ABOVE ON TOP.

YOU MAY REDEEM THE COUPONS BY SENDING THEM TO:

PALISADES CUSTOMER SERVICE
QUESTAR PUBLISHERS, INC.
P.O. BOX 1720
SISTERS, OR 97759

CANADIANS SEND TO:
BEACON DISTRIBUTING
P.O. BOX 98
PARIS, ONTARIO
N3L 3E5

BUY SIX
GET ONE
FREE

PALISADES
FREQUENT
BUYER
COUPON

Applies to any Palisades novel priced at $8.99 and below.

Dealer must retain coupon from free Palisades novel.

Consumer must pay any applicable sales tax.

AT PARTICIPATING DEALERS

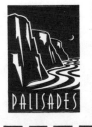

PALISADES